Digital Innovation Adoption: Architectural Recommendations and Security Solutions

Edited By

Muhammad Ehsan Rana
School of Computer Science
Asia Pacific University of Technology & Innovation
Kuala Lumpur
Malaysia

&

Manoj Jayabalan
School of Computer Science & Mathematics
Liverpool John Moores University
Liverpool
UK

Digital Innovation Adoption: Architectural Recommendations and Security Solutions

Editors: Muhammad Ehsan Rana & Manoj Jayabalan

ISBN (Online): 978-981-5079-66-1

ISBN (Print): 978-981-5079-67-8

ISBN (Paperback): 978-981-5079-68-5

First published in 2024.

General:

1. Any dispute or claim arising out of or in connection with this License Agreement or the Work (including non-contractual disputes or claims) will be governed by and construed in accordance with the laws of the U.A.E. as applied in the Emirate of Dubai. Each party agrees that the courts of the Emirate of Dubai shall have exclusive jurisdiction to settle any dispute or claim arising out of or in connection with this License Agreement or the Work (including non-contractual disputes or claims).
2. Your rights under this License Agreement will automatically terminate without notice and without the need for a court order if at any point you breach any terms of this License Agreement. In no event will any delay or failure by Bentham Science Publishers in enforcing your compliance with this License Agreement constitute a waiver of any of its rights.
3. You acknowledge that you have read this License Agreement, and agree to be bound by its terms and conditions. To the extent that any other terms and conditions presented on any website of Bentham Science Publishers conflict with, or are inconsistent with, the terms and conditions set out in this License Agreement, you acknowledge that the terms and conditions set out in this License Agreement shall prevail.

Bentham Science Publishers Ltd.
Executive Suite Y - 2
PO Box 7917, Saif Zone
Sharjah, U.A.E.
Email: subscriptions@benthamscience.org

CONTENTS

FOREWORD

I am delighted to write this foreword because I believe deeply in the importance of the topics and of high quality of the contents. There is latest and so much useful information being delivered into its 15 chapters which should not be missed. Thus it gives me a great pleasure to contribute this foreword.

As I reviewed the manuscript prior to writing this foreword, I was impressed by many unique features that I would like to share with you. The book explores the important aspect of the architectural requirements including emerging technologies and security-based concerns for digital innovation adoption. This work would be an important resource of exposure towards the Internet-of-Thing (IoT) and Artificial Intelligence (AI) in various important application domains.

Smart Cities and 5G Networks highlighted the advantages and disadvantages of radio and device-to-device in the context of multiple IoT use cases. IoT in Waste Management introduced an intelligent smart bin system to automate waste handling and management to contribute to green technology. Stock Monitoring System Using IoT Based Automation provided a set of recommendations for a hypermarket stock monitoring system using IoT automation. Secure Healthcare Using Blockchain Technology reviewed blockchain architecture in a health domain in order to secure patients' medical records. E-Voting System Using Blockchain Technology implemented blockchain for e-voting systems of medium and large-scale size.

Decentralised News Using Blockchain Technology explained the implementation of blockchain via a decentralised application to combat misinformation. Cyber Threats in IoT-based Connected Cars exposed vulnerabilities for IoT-based connected cars and their implications. The use of IoT in Contact Tracing: Vulnerabilities and Countermeasures reviewed contact tracing application with IoT. AI-based Intrusion Detection System for IoT Security proposed a solution for security treats for IoT network with Intrusion Detection System. Fake News Detection Using Data Mining Approaches introduced a data mining as a technique to predict fake news.

EEG Signal Classification Using AI Techniques analysed the classification methods for EEG signals. Malware Analysis and Malicious Activity Detection Using Machine Learning reviewed AI techniques to protect and prevent security threats in the IT infrastructure. Interestingly the authors have proposed a machine-learning based detection system to classify suspicious objects. Security Vulnerabilities and Threats for IoT-based Home revealed the security vulnerabilities for the smart home concept and its protection. IoT Policy and Governance Reference Architecture discussed IoT reference architecture, policy and governance for the integrity and security of the information being transmitted within the IoT ecosystem. Organizational Security Improvement in Preventing Deepfake Ransomware highlighted the impact of deep fake ransomware to the organisation and its protection.

The content provides a widely useful compilation of ideas, cases, innovative approaches, and practical strategies for enhancing digital innovation adoption mainly covering the architecture and security. This book should be read by anyone including researchers, educators, industry practitioners and technology specialists who intend to learn, practice, and adopt innovative technology in their respective areas of interest to bring digital transformation by indulging in the architectural requirements and security concerns.

Wan Nurhayati Wan Ab. Rahman, Ph.D
Faculty of Computer Science and Information Technology
Universiti Putra Malaysia
Selangor
Malaysia

PREFACE

Digital innovation assists organizations in innovating and driving services to bespoke clients that leverage high value. The integration of major disruptive technologies such as cloud, big data, IoT and blockchain has ignited the retransformation of the entire industrial arena. As a result of this convergence of technologies, organisations need to go through a mandatory process of change at a rapid pace. Every industry, from agriculture to manufacturing, transportation to education, pharmaceutical to health services, is forced to be revolutionised using innovative approaches. Organisation's products, services, and operations need to embrace a technological shift to differentiate themselves in the competitive arena and satisfy their customers' ever-increasing needs. Billions of digitally enabled devices will create the dawn of a whole new era by utilising their sensing, processing, and connectivity power through the use of the Internet of Things (IoT). Consumer-based companies rely heavily on mobile devices to deliver personal experiences. Cloud is redefining the way businesses were previously done. It is a paradigm shift from traditional IT to a more efficient, scalable, and secure infrastructure. Blockchain offers a decentralised structure that demonstrates transparency and trust and provides individual control of data. Organisations need to lay down the sophisticated architectural requirements of the proposed solutions to take advantage of the evolving digital technology. The extensive reliance on these technologies has also possessed some security challenges for providers and consumers. The ubiquitous data access *via* multiple end-user devices has paved the way for security and cyber threats. As information security is critical for contemporary businesses, organisations have an essential role in protecting the information to deal with highly augmented security and privacy threats. This book is intended to explore the architectural requirements of these digitally transformed systems by adopting emerging technologies and examining security-based concerns considering the vulnerabilities and countermeasures for these systems.

Muhammad Ehsan Rana
School of Computer Science
Asia Pacific University of Technology & Innovation
Kuala Lumpur
Malaysia

&

Manoj Jayabalan
School of Computer Science & Mathematics
Liverpool John Moores University
Liverpool
UK

List of Contributors

Attique Ur Rehman	School of System and Technology, University of Management and Technology, Pakistan
Ainkaran Doraisamy	School of Computing & Technology, Asia Pacific University of Technology and Innovation, Kuala Lumpur, Malaysia
Abdullah Khalid	School of Computing & Technology, Asia Pacific University of Technology and Innovation, Kuala Lumpur, Malaysia
Daniel Mago Vistro	School of Computing, Asia Pacific University, Kuala Lumpur, Malaysia
Intan Farahana Kamsin	School of Computing & Technology, Asia Pacific University of Technology and Innovation, Kuala Lumpur, Malaysia
Janesh Kapoor	School of Computing & Technology, Asia Pacific University of Technology and Innovation, Kuala Lumpur, Malaysia
Julia Juremi	Forensic and Cyber Security Research Center, Asia Pacific University of Technology and Innovation, Kuala Lumpur, Malaysia
Khalida Shajaratuddur Harun	School of Computing & Technology, Asia Pacific University of Technology and Innovation, Kuala Lumpur, Malaysia
Maryam Var Naseri	School of Computing & Technology, Asia Pacific University of Technology and Innovation, Kuala Lumpur, Malaysia
Muhammad Shoaib Farooq	School of System and Technology, University of Management and Technology, Pakistan
Muhammad Jawed Chowdhury	School of Computing & Technology, Asia Pacific University of Technology and Innovation, Kuala Lumpur, Malaysia
Manoj Jayabalan	School of Computer Science and Mathematics, Liverpool John Moores University, Liverpool, UK
Nor Azlina Abdul Rahman	Forensic and Cyber Security Research Centre, Asia Pacific University of Technology and Innovation, Kuala Lumpur, Malaysia
Nur Khairunnisha Zainal	School of Computing & Technology, Asia Pacific University of Technology and Innovation, Kuala Lumpur, Malaysia
Shiksha	School of Computer Science and Mathematics, Liverpool John Moores University, Liverpool, UK
Waleed Zafar	School of System and Technology, University of Management and Technology, Pakistan
Yap Chi Yew	School of Computing & Technology, Asia Pacific University of Technology and Innovation, Kuala Lumpur, Malaysia

CHAPTER 1

Access and Secure Patient Medical Records using Blockchain Technology based Framework: A Review

Daniel Mago Vistro[1,*], **Muhammad Shoaib Farooq**[2], **Attique Ur Rehman**[2] and **Waleed Zafar**[2]

[1] *School of Computing, Asia Pacific University, Kuala Lumpur, Malaysia*

[2] *School of System and Technology, University of Management and Technology, Pakistan*

Abstract: Blockchain technology has a key role in electronic health record systems for storing, accessing and securing patients' medical records. Patients' medical information is being stored like personal bio, diagnosis, treatments, *etc.* This information is very sensitive and private, and it has remained a big challenge to access and secure patient medical records in a decentralized manner. Blockchain has become very important for its use in storing, accessing and managing patient medical records in a very secure and decentralized manner. In this paper, a systematic literature review has been done to review blockchain architecture for electronic health records systems to store, access and secure patient medical records. The main objective of this paper is to highlight the use of blockchain in accessing and securing patient medical records. Moreover, some blockchain-based electronic health records systems have been presented to secure the records. Lastly, some challenges and gaps in using blockchain-based medical health records systems have been presented.

Keywords: Block Chain, Centralized, Electronic health records, Framework, Patient medical records, Technology.

1. INTRODUCTION

Patient medical records contain very important information about a patient's health history, medications, and allergies. This information is used by many health care providers and research institutes to provide better care and to conduct research that can lead to new treatments and cures [2]. Different institutions are using the technology to save and secure patient information, but private patient data security is the main issue [3]. The data for patients like personal information,

* **Corresponding author Daniel Mago Vistro:** School of Computing, Asia Pacific University, Kuala Lumpur, Malaysia; E-mail: Daniel.mago@apu.edu.my

Muhammad Ehsan Rana & Manoj Jayabalan (Eds.)

diagnosis, treatments, symptoms, region, *etc.*, is growing with the passage of time. Patient medical record systems that store and manage patient data are being used by different institutions, and it is becoming an important technology [4]. There are many stakeholders that are involved in managing and accessing patient data. But it has with many challenges like data insecurity and accessibility [5]. Patients need to visit different hospitals, clinics or any health care system for medical diagnosis, treatments *etc*, in such cases, patient data sharing is important for better treatment and medications [4]. The patient does not have access to their medical records, which could make it difficult for them to get the care they need. Additionally, patient data can be shared with an unauthorized person or stolen, which could lead to identity theft or other problems.

Blockchain technology is becoming more important these days because it provides many features like decentralized immutability and security of data [1]. Blockchain technology is being used in electronic health record systems that help share the data of patients among many stakeholders. Through blockchain technology, a patient can control who can access the data. It provides security to data by using its advanced algorithms [6].

In this paper, we have presented how blockchain technologies help to improve patient data accessibility and security in electronic health record systems. We have described the architecture of blockchain to understand its working and how it can help to improve the current patient records system. The challenges and gaps in using blockchain have also been presented in this article.

2. RELATED WORK

Patient information is highly sensitive and private; it is being shared with multiple stakeholders. The challenge is to secure the information by using emerging technology such as blockchain because it is quite considerable due to its highly secured hashing algorithms. A survey has been done on the use of blockchain in healthcare that discusses accessibility, security and privacy challenges in electronic health records [2]. However, the challenges in using blockchain-based record systems have not been discussed. The role of blockchain technology has been discussed in telehealth and telemedicine [7]. But the blockchain architecture has not been presented for managing patient records. A systematic literature review of blockchain for electronic health records systems has been done [6] for the security and privacy challenges. However, the security architecture has not been discussed. The use of information in health care by using blockchain technology has been discussed in a study [8]. They have discussed the challenges that affect the transition of patient information. A systematic review has been done on using of blockchain applications in the health sector. But the blockchain architecture has not been presented.

The novelty in this paper is that we have focused on the role of blockchain in patient medical records in the sense of storing and sharing data. Our study focuses on the security of patient data by using the blockchain. We have discussed the challenges and gaps of blockchain-based electronic health records in this paper.

3. RESEARCH METHODOLOGY

A systematic literature view method has been selected for this paper to review the use of block technologies framework to ensure the availability and security of patient records. The objectives of this review are to provide an overview of how blockchain methods are helping to improve the accessibility and security of patient records in a system. We have used the proposed method by Kai Petersen [9]. We have followed the steps as mentioned in Fig. (**1**).

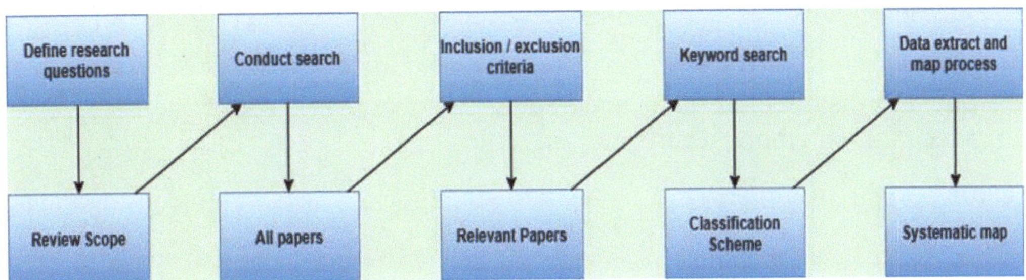

Fig. (1). Steps to conduct a systematic review.

4. RESEARCH OBJECTIVE

The objectives of this research are:

RO1. The main focus is to highlight the use of blockchain methods in accessing, securing managing patient medical records.

RO2. Improving the security of patient medical records while using blockchain.

RO3. Explore challenges and gaps in using blockchain-based electronic health record systems.

5. RESEARCH QUESTION

The important thing in systematic literature views is defining the research questions. After reading a detailed literature review, we have defined the following questions as in Table (**1**).

Table 1. Research questions.

Q. No	Questions	Motivation
Q1	Why is a decentralized blockchain patient record system better than centralized patient record systems?	Role of blockchain-based health record systems
Q2	How will blockchain ensure that patient records are secure and traceable?	Explore the important characteristics of smart contracts in blockchain
Q3	What are the challenges and gaps in using blockchain-based electronic health records?	Describe the challenges in using blockchain for electronic health record

Q1. Why is a decentralized blockchain patient record system better than centralized patient record systems?

This review enables us to explore the blockchain role in storing, accessing and securing patient medical records.

Q2. How will blockchain ensure that patient records are secure and traceable?

This question has helped us to understand the characteristics of the blockchain that makes the data more secure and traceable.

Q3. What are the challenges and gaps in using blockchain-based electronic health records?

This question enables us to review the challenges and gaps in using blockchain for patient health records.

6. CONDUCTING SEARCH

This is the second step of the systematic literature view to search the papers related to a research topic. The search string has been identified to collect the articles using different repositories. The papers are searched from different databases, including Springer Link, IEEE Xplore, Science Direct and ACM digital library. The following combination has been used to define the search string; refer to Table (**2**).

$\forall$ Primary $\wedge$ Secondary $\vee$ $\forall$ Additional

Table 2. Search strategy.

Database	Search String
Springer Link	("Patient Medical Records" OR "Electronic medical record" OR "Patient data") AND ("Blockchain" OR "Blockchain technology" OR "Blockchain security") AND ("ehealth" OR "telehealth" OR "healthcare") Publication Year: Year 2018-2020
IEEE Xplore	("Patient Medical Records" OR "Electronic medical record" OR "Patient data") AND ("Blockchain" OR "Blockchain technology" OR "Blockchain security") AND ("ehealth" OR "telehealth" OR "healthcare") Publication Year: Year 2018-2020
Science Direct	("Patient Medical Records" OR "Electronic medical record" OR "Patient data") AND ("Blockchain" OR "Blockchain technology" OR "Blockchain security") AND ("ehealth" OR "telehealth" OR "healthcare") Publication Year: Year 2018-2020
ACM digital library	("Patient Medical Records" OR "Electronic medical record" OR "Patient data") AND ("Blockchain" OR "Blockchain technology" OR "Blockchain security") AND ("ehealth" OR "telehealth" OR "healthcare") Publication Year: Year 2018-2020

7. INCLUSION AND EXCLUSION CRITERIA

We have included papers that were:

- Related to the search string
- Papers that are published from 2018 -2020
- That contains blockchain techniques
- Related to patient medical records

We have excluded the following articles:

- The titles were not matched with the blockchain and patient medical records
- Books
- Without abstract
- Does not contain blockchain solutions.

8. SEARCH AND RESULTS AND COLLECTION

The initial results retrieved were 2447 against the search string on databases. The results of the search and selection of research papers are shown in Table (**3**). The papers were included or excluded based on titles. We examined the titles of all papers, and the result was 314. Many papers were not related to the topic, so we excluded those. After applying inclusion and exclusion criteria, we selected 18 papers for this research paper.

Table 3. Search and selection process.

Sr.	Process	Criteria Used	ACM Digital Library	Springer	Science Direct	IEEE Explore	Total Results
1	General Search	By keywords	981	759	568	139	2447
2	First round of screening	Removed based on titles	59	211	21	23	314
3	Second round of screening	Abstracts	13	24	11	4	52
4	Final selection	Entire article	3	7	4	4	18

9. KEYWORDING

In this, we have done the keywording process on the basis of abstracts. We have used the process defined by Petersen [9]. We have examined the abstracts and basic concepts of contribution related to the topic. Keywords have been identified as primary, secondary and additional, as shown in Fig (**2**).

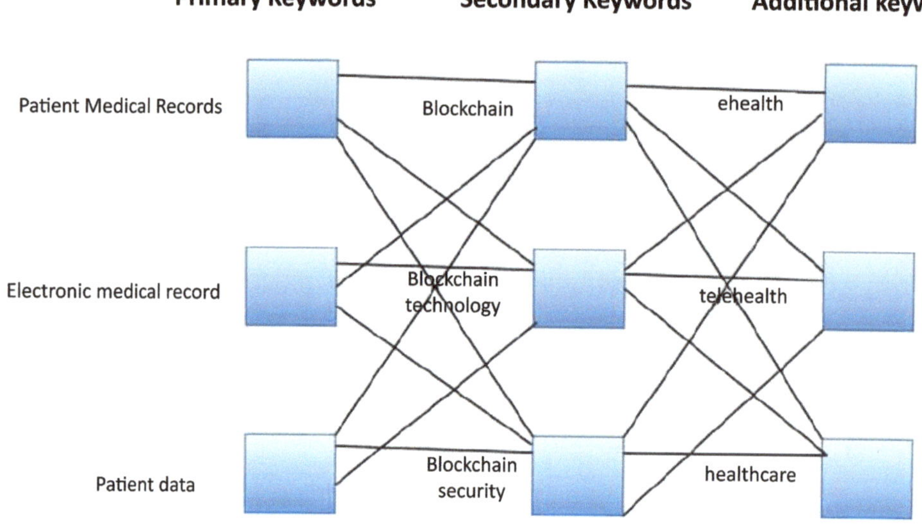

Fig. (2). Search String Keywording.

10. QUALITY ASSESSMENT

The quality assessment criteria have been identified to check or assess the quality of selected papers. We have defined some questions to score the paper quality as in Table (**4**).

Table 4. Criteria for Quality Assessment.

Criteria	Ranking	Score
The papers provide a clear solution or contribution for the role of blockchain in managing patient medical records	Yes No	1 0
The methods for using blockchain was clearly explained	Yes No	1 0
Databases ranking Journals / Conference	Q1 Q2 Q3 Core A Core B Core C	2.5 2 1.5 2 1.5 1

11. DATA EXTRACTION AND CLASSIFICATION

This process was followed to get the possible answers to the questions that are already defined in Table **1**. All information related to addressing the questions was retrieved in these steps, including the title of the paper, authors, and journal information. The initial search retrieved 2,447 results. After removing duplications and screening the titles, the result was 314. Then the second phase of screening was done based on abstracts of the papers, and the result was 52. The final selected article for this paper is 18. Table **3** shows the selection process from different scientific databases.

12. ASSESSMENTS OF RESEARCH QUESTIONS

Q1. Why is the decentralized blockchain patient record system better than the centralized patient record systems?

Patient data may have been compromised when using the centralized health record systems. As blockchain is peer to peer and decentralized technology, it has an important role in electronic health records. Many techniques are being used to make the data more secure and traceable. Through blockchain, access is given to patients to control their medical records in one place and provide security [10]. As blockchain, main features include shared immutable and transparency for all the transactions, enabling the stakeholder to provide an opportunity to use EMR systems based on blockchain [11].

Smart contracts ensure the security of data in a blockchain-based system. Consensus algorithms have been imposed to verify and secure the records in a system. Blockchain methods help us [12]. The patient data cannot be accessed by unauthorized entities. Any change or malicious attack can be tracked or traced using blockchain-based health records systems. The patient will have control over their own data. The security can be managed, and tracking of data sharing is possible.

The decentralization feature provides a decentralized system, which means there will be no central entity. So all the entities in blockchain will have equal rights to read/write data [13]. Every block has the previous block hash value, so if any block data is changed, then the hash values of each block will be recalculated, and that node will be invalid [14]. The private information of entities is being encrypted and open to all, so those who have permission will query the data and have access to the information.

Q2. How will blockchain ensure that patient records are secure and traceable?

Patient information privacy may be compromised if the data is leaked in electronic health record systems. Blockchain provides us secure immutability and transparency by implementing its techniques in health records systems [11]. In Fig (**3**), a blockchain-based system has been defined along with its process in a study [15]. The process is simply described. All the participants register through the application and ask the service provider for the certificate. The service provider will issue the certificate and will assign a key along with the ID. The transactions are sent to the EHR ledger. The providers can access only those records that have been allowed to them. When a record is updated, it is distributed to all the participants over the blockchain, so every node has the same copy of data every time, so it is not possible to alter or delete the data. Each transaction has a previous hash value along with the timestamp, so history is being recorded. It makes the system more secure [15].

Another blockchain-based system has been proposed by [16].

MedChain: (A blockchain-based health record system) [16] Eman-Yasser proposed a blockchain-based for managing patient records system that is called MedChain. The main purpose of this system is to enable security effectiveness for the records. It keeps the privacy of patients on priority. Smart contracts have been employed in this system for the transactions and access control to health records. For security purposes, the encryption methodology has been adopted. They have employed hashing algorithm SHA-256 to ensure data security and integrity. When a record is saved in an electrical health system, Medchain keeps the hash value of that record. This encrypted value will be sent to an authorized person to access the data. This value is unique, so it makes sure that no one can change or alter the data.

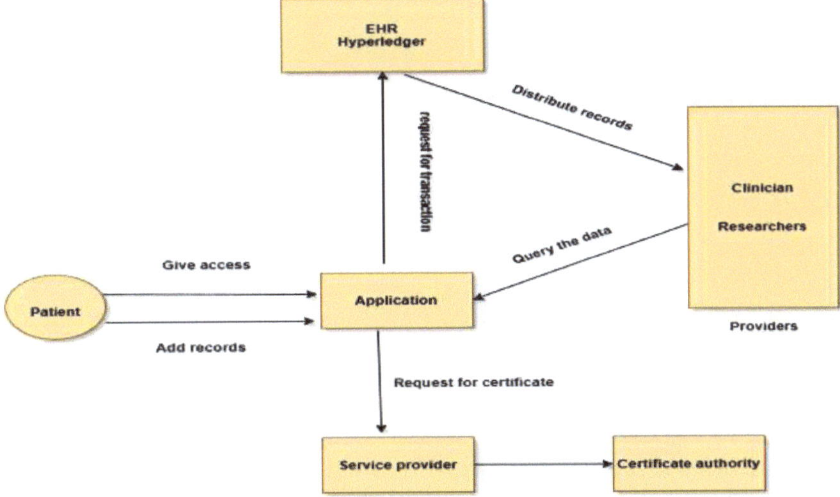

Fig. (3). Blockchain-based EHR system.

To ensure security, MedChain stores the hash value, key and record in different locations. To maintain privacy, smart contracts have been used in this system. For the validation of new blocks or records, the Proof of Authority algorithm has been used to verify the new records [8].

Proof of Authority Algorithm helps us to create authorities in a blockchain that will have access to add the data and will ensure the security of data [13]. The re-encryption technique encrypts messages or data in a way that allows the other entity to decrypt them with their private key. Smart contracts are used to ensure that authorized transactions have been performed [17]. They monitor all transactions in the chain [18]. These are sets of functions that execute when certain conditions are met. Above all, protocols help to make the patient records storing, sharing and accessibility decentralized. All have their own unique function to enhance data security and assure the privacy of patients private information.

Above all, protocols help to make the patient records storing, sharing and accessibility decentralized. All have their own unique function to enhance data security and assure the privacy of patients private information.

Another keyless signature framework has been proposed by [14] to ensure the data security of health records. It uses the hash function to secure the data.

Q3. What are the challenges and gaps in using blockchain-based electronic health records?

Blockchain comes with massive benefits and opportunities, but it still has some challenges and issues when applying it in managing patient medical records [19].

13. SCALABILITY

One of the challenges is storage capacity. There is a lot of patient data that needs to be stored on the blockchain, including personal information, diagnosis, treatments that may contain a lot of images as well. Data is becoming larger every day, and it has no limit. This will increase the size of the database that may lower the process of accessing or searching the data. So we need a scalability solution for a blockchain [5].

14. STANDARDS

The standardization of the blockchain is still a challenge. Standards for every industry has not been identified yet. There is a lack of knowledge about the type of data and its accessibility. There is a need to define the standard of information sharing, the format of data, size evaluation in blockchain for health care applications [19].

15. TRANSFORMATION

Many health care sectors are using blockchain applications for patient records management, but still, there is a challenge to motivate clinical persons to use the blockchain rather than paperwork or centralized applications [7]. The old systems have been used over the years, and it is very difficult to transform them on a blockchain. There will be a need for more expertise and knowledge to store and access the data through blockchain-based health records applications.

16. COMPLEXITY DISCUSSION

We conducted a systematic literature review to provide a detailed discussion of how blockchain-based electronic health records systems can help in accessing and securing patient medical records. A model is proposed in Fig (**4**) to summarize the results of this article.

Proposed model for Electronic health records.

This model uses two blockchain schemes, one is a private blockchain, and the other is a consortium blockchain. The private block saves all the data of patient medical records, and the consortium chain contains indexes of the private records. The data will be stored on different nodes. When a user requests data, the identity of the user is checked through different algorithms techniques. After the user verification, the requested information is sent to the user. For security purpose, all record and patient identity is encrypted with the public key. This makes the data more secure in a blockchain.

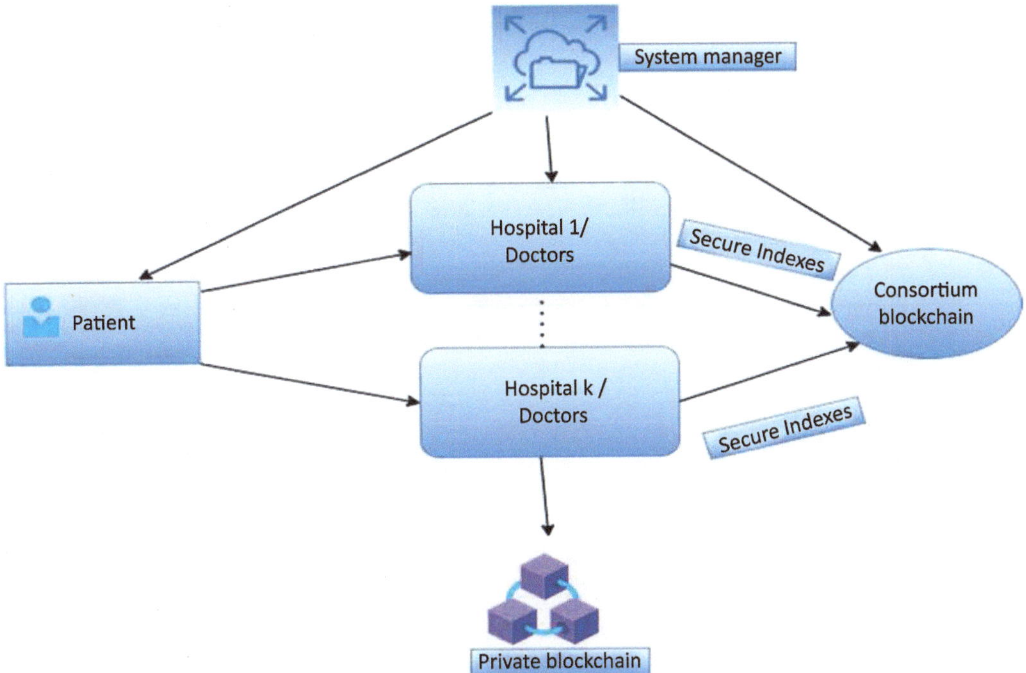

Fig. (4). Proposed Model for Electronic Health Records.

CONCLUSION

In this paper, a systematic literature review has been done to identify the use of blockchain in storing, accessing and securing patient medical records. This study has been conducted by selecting 18 articles, and we have gone through all the processes of systematic literature review. Patients' private information cannot be compromised in the sense of security and privacy. So, there was a need to highlight the important features of blockchain that are being used for storing, sharing and accessing patient information. We have reviewed some blockchain features that can be implemented to make the patient data secure and stored in a decentralized manner so it can be accessed by authorized users easily. We have reviewed different blockchain-based patient records systems that use different algorithms to make the data secure and accessible to all authorized entities. We have also discussed challenges and gaps in using blockchain applications in health care systems. We conclude that using blockchain-based systems for managing patients' medical records makes these records easily accessible, traceable, and secure.

REFERENCES

[1] S.G. Alonso, J. Arambarri, M. López-Coronado, and I. de la Torre Díez, "Proposing New Blockchain Challenges in eHealth", *J. Med. Syst.,* vol. 43, no. 3, p. 64, 2019. [http://dx.doi.org/10.1007/s10916-019-1195-7] [PMID: 30729329]

[2] M. Sookhak, M.R. Jabbarpour, N.S. Safa, and F.R. Yu, "Blockchain and smart contract for access control in healthcare: A survey, issues and challenges, and open issues", *J. Netw. Comput. Appl.,* vol. 178, p. 102950, 2021. [http://dx.doi.org/10.1016/j.jnca.2020.102950]

[3] K. Fan, S. Wang, Y. Ren, H. Li, and Y. Yang, "MedBlock: Efficient and secure medical data sharing *via* blockchain", *J. Med. Syst.,* vol. 42, no. 8, p. 136, 2018. [http://dx.doi.org/10.1007/s10916-018-0993-7] [PMID: 29931655]

[4] D.M. Vistro, A.U. Rehman, M.S. Farooq, A. Abid, and M. Idrees, "A literature review on security issues in cloud computing: Opportunities and challenges", *J. Crit. Rev.,* vol. 7, no. 10, pp. 1446-1455, 2020. [http://dx.doi.org/10.31838/jcr.07.10.282]

[5] N.S. Khan, A. Abid, K. Abid, U. Farooq, M.S. Farooq, and H. Jameel, "Speak Pakistan: Challenges in developing Pakistan sign language using information technology", *South Asian Stud.,* vol. 30, no. 2, 2020. Corpus ID: 21208581

[6] S. Shi, D. He, L. Li, N. Kumar, M.K. Khan, and K.K.R. Choo, "Applications of blockchain in ensuring the security and privacy of electronic health record systems: A survey", *Comput. Secur.,* vol. 97, p. 101966, 2020. [http://dx.doi.org/10.1016/j.cose.2020.101966] [PMID: 32834254]

[7] R.W. Ahmad, K. Salah, R. Jayaraman, I. Yaqoob, S. Ellahham, and M. Omar, "The role of blockchain technology in telehealth and telemedicine", *Int. J. Med. Inform.,* vol. 148, p. 104399, 2021. [http://dx.doi.org/10.1016/j.ijmedinf.2021.104399] [PMID: 33540131]

[8] W.J. Gordon, and C. Catalini, "Blockchain Technology for Healthcare: Facilitating the Transition to Patient-Driven Interoperability", *Comput. Struct. Biotechnol. J.,* vol. 16, pp. 224-230, 2018. [http://dx.doi.org/10.1016/j.csbj.2018.06.003] [PMID: 30069284]

[9] K. Petersen, R. Feldt, S. Mujtaba, and M. Mattsson, "Systematic mapping studies in software engineering", *12th International Conference on Evaluation and Assessment in Software Engineering (EASE) (EASE),* 2008. [http://dx.doi.org/10.14236/ewic/EASE2008.8]

[10] D.M. Vistro, A.U. Rehman, M.S. Farooq, A. Abid, and M. Idrees, "A survey on cloud computing security with cross-platform", *J. Critic. Rev.,* vol. 7, no. 10, pp. 1439-1445, 2020.

[11] A. Dubovitskaya, Z. Xu, S.Ryu, M. Schumacher, F. Wang. "Secure and Trustable Electronic Medical Records Sharing using Blockchain" *AMIA. Annu. Symp. Proc.* pp. 650-659, 2018. https://pubmed.ncbi.nlm.nih.gov/29854130

[12] X. Liu, Z. Wang, C. Jin, F. Li, and G. Li, "A blockchain-based medical data sharing and protection scheme", *IEEE Access,* vol. 7, pp. 118943-118953, 2019. [http://dx.doi.org/10.1109/ACCESS.2019.2937685]

[13] M. Belotti, N. Božić, G. Pujolle, and S. Secci, "A Vademecum on Blockchain Technologies: When, Which, and How", *IEEE Commun. Surv. Tutor.,* vol. 21, no. 4, pp. 3796-3838, 2019. [http://dx.doi.org/10.1109/COMST.2019.2928178]

[14] G. Nagasubramanian, R.K. Sakthivel, R. Patan, A.H. Gandomi, M. Sankayya, and B. Balusamy, "Securing e-health records using keyless signature infrastructure blockchain technology in the cloud", *Neural Comput. Appl.,* vol. 32, no. 3, pp. 639-647, 2020. [http://dx.doi.org/10.1007/s00521-018-3915-1]

[15] S. Tanwar, K. Parekh, and R. Evans, "Blockchain-based electronic healthcare record system for healthcare 4.0 applications", *J. Inf. Secur. Appl.*, vol. 50, p. 102407, 2020. [http://dx.doi.org/10.1016/j.jisa.2019.102407]

[16] E.Y. Daraghmi, Y.A. Daraghmi, and S.M. Yuan, "MedChain: a design of a blockchain-based system for medical records access and permissions management", *IEEE Access,* vol. 7, pp. 164595-164613, 2019. [http://dx.doi.org/10.1109/ACCESS.2019.2952942]

[17] A. Zhang, and X. Lin, "Towards Secure and Privacy-Preserving Data Sharing in e-Health Systems *via* Consortium Blockchain", *J. Med. Syst.,* vol. 42, no. 8, p. 140, 2018. [http://dx.doi.org/10.1007/s10916-018-0995-5] [PMID: 29956061]

[18] N. Kshetri, "Blockchain and Electronic Healthcare Records [Cybertrust]", *Computer,* vol. 51, no. 12, pp. 59-63, 2018. [http://dx.doi.org/10.1109/MC.2018.2880021]

[19] A.A. Siyal, A.Z. Junejo, M. Zawish, K. Ahmed, A. Khalil, and G. Soursou, "Applications of Blockchain Technology in Medicine and Healthcare: Challenges and Future Perspectives", *Cryptography,* vol. 3, no. 1, p. 3, 2019. [http://dx.doi.org/10.3390/cryptography3010003]

CHAPTER 2

Identifying Cyber Threats in IoT based Connected Cars for Enhanced Security

Ainkaran Doraisamy[1], **Nor Azlina Abdul Rahman**[2,*] and **Khalida Shajaratuddur Harun**[1]

[1] *School of Computing & Technology, Asia Pacific University of Technology and Innovation, Kuala Lumpur, Malaysia*

[2] *Forensic and Cyber Security Research Centre, Asia Pacific University of Technology and Innovation, Kuala Lumpur, Malaysia*

Abstract: The Internet of Things (IoT) has garnered many ideas to create new IoT products as well as enhance their existing products with the help of the internet. Tesla is an example of an IoT device from the automotive industry. The most prominent feature of the vehicle was the over-the-air (OTA) updates. A few vulnerabilities were found in Tesla despite being one of the most secure vehicles in the world. The first vulnerability was in the vehicle's key system, where radio signals from the key fob were intercepted in a relay attack. The next vulnerability was due to the Tesla app, where the hacker obtained the owner's login credentials. Besides, the infotainment system of the vehicle also was compromised and hacked using a web browser bug known as a JIT bug. Lastly, Tesla vehicles also had a vulnerability in their navigation system too. This was demonstrated by a group of researchers who staged a GPS spoof attack on Tesla model 3 while it was in Autopilot mode. Fake satellite coordinates were transmitted by the researchers, who were then received by the GPS receiver. This caused the vehicle to decelerate and made an emergency turn-off at a narrow pit stop. These vulnerabilities can be fixed by following safety measures to counter cyber-attacks. More layers of security should be installed on the existing security system to ensure the vehicle does not get exploited easily by hackers.

Keywords: Cyber attacks, Internet of things, IoT vulnerabilities, Key fob, Smart car application and IoT defence.

* **Corresponding author Nor Azlina Abdul Rahman:** Forensic and Cyber Security Research Centre, Asia Pacific University of Technology & Innovation, Kuala Lumpur, Malaysia; E-mail: nor_azlina@apu.edu.my

Muhammad Ehsan Rana & Manoj Jayabalan (Eds.)

1. INTRODUCTION

The purpose of IoT is to enable simple things to be connected to the internet in order to gather and exchange data that does not require much human or computer involvement. With IoT, the power of the internet can be extended to a wide range of things such as bottles, mugs, watches, coffee makers and many more. It converts an existing object into a "smart" object in which these things are able to send and receive information. This adds additional value to these objects since more features and opportunities can be unlocked from the objects that make them multifunctional.

Industries have come up with many ideas to create new IoT products as well as to enhance their existing products by implementing and recreating a "smart" product with the help of the internet. There are many advantages of IoT, such as creating more business opportunities. Advanced analytics can be used to obtain insights related to business which may assist in reducing costs on operations. IoT is capable of predicting an issue and acting before it occurs. This is because the network of IoT is able to provide insights from the collected data, which may help to reduce or even prevent maintenance issues or system breakdowns. IoT can also be used as a way to further improvise their products and services to customers. The utilisation of IoT can be a turning point for almost any industry or organisation since it helps to elevate the products or services according to customers' needs [1].

The top 10 IoT application areas in 2020.

The transportation or automotive industry is ranked second in this analysis. It is also evident that the use of IoT in this industry shows a positive trend. In the automotive industry, connected cars are vehicles that run on their own internet connection. Tesla cars are one such prominent example of IoT devices in this industry. There are many applications of IoT in Tesla cars [2]. In terms of connectivity, Tesla has a standard 3G mobile connection that connects the car to the internet, which is free for its users for navigating purposes. Features and the search results for maps are sorted and organised according to distance. Apart from that, there is also a package for premium connectivity in which Tesla car owners are able to gain access to many other applications such as visuals of live traffics, streaming of media and music using Spotify while driving and Netflix as well as YouTube applications while the car is parked. There are also other built-in features such as Bluetooth and Homelink, which automatically control gates, garage doors, lights and even a home security system [3].

Besides, Tesla has an API that helps the owners to lock or unlock their car, to find their car and also to read data. This can be done by installing a Smart car application and connecting their car to it. By doing this, the car can be locked or unlocked using the mobile application with just some codes lines. Another unique feature of Tesla is that it has Over the Air (OTA) updates. OTA enables the vehicle to update its software versions automatically. These updates are done on the cars on a regular basis to improve the performance and safety of the car. Some of the updates include upgrading the existing design features such as the touchscreen, which are upgraded by modifying the look of it in order to satisfy their customers. OTA updates help to reduce visits to the dealer for maintenance purposes as well as save cost and time. Furthermore, Tesla collects all the performance data of their cars and monitors each car. According to the data collected, if any car needs further maintenance, Tesla would contact the owner to inform and schedule a slot for maintenance of the car [4]. These large amounts of data also will be used by engineers in Tesla for further improvements and to track the driving patterns of their customers. There are sensors in the car that enable screening of the driver to detect and track any reckless driving pattern which might be caused by factors such as the level of fatigue. The monitoring system will then take control of the car speed in order to prevent road accidents.

This system is made up of components such as alcohol, impact and eye blink sensors which are used to locate the car with the help of Google Maps. This system can also be used to detect the exact location of stolen cars by using GPS. The server of the application will receive satellite signals according to the coordinates of the location, and the vehicle owner can be notified and informed after tracking the location of the car, (Fig. **1**).

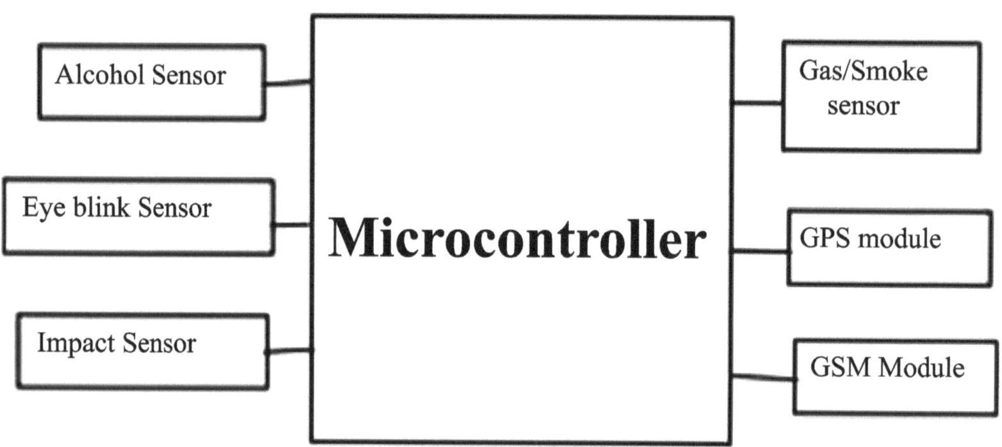

Fig. (1). Monitoring system of a car [4].

2. VULNERABILITIES

There are a few vulnerabilities that can be found in a Tesla despite being one of the most secured cars in the world. Hackers tend to use these vulnerabilities to take advantage of and exploit the system. The first vulnerability is the vehicle's key system [5].

Table **1** shows the type of key systems that are used by cars. Tesla is equipped with a Passive Keyless Entry and Start (PKES) system in its key fob. Key fob is a device that contains built-in authentication for locking and unlocking the car within a specific range of distance from the car. Most key fobs contain a transponder that works by depending on radio-frequency identification or also known as RFID. This is what enables the vehicle to either unlock or lock and also to carry out its other functions. The encrypted signals and the frequency from the key fob can be decoded within a matter of seconds because the encryption used to build the key fob is manufactured with encryption that is not sophisticated. Once the signals are decoded, the message between the car and the key can be relayed. The hacker will then proceed to take control of the car and drive away in it right after unlocking and starting it. This is called a relay attack. Some of them even manage to discover ways to disable certain access in which even location tracking of the car can be disabled. This can lead to an increase in cases related to car thefts [4].

Table 1. Type of key-systems in cars [4].

Denomination	Entry	Start Engine
Physical key with RFID immobiliser	Physical key	Physical key
Keyless entry with RFID immobiliser	Remote active	Physical key + RFID
Passive keyless entry and start	Remote passive	Remote passive

The next vulnerability is the Tesla application itself, and this is because the Tesla app on an Android smartphone is not that secured [6]. Tesla app plays a fundamental role as it is used to monitor and control Tesla. Almost 90 per cent of Android smartphones are exposed to vulnerability due to outdated software. This is done by hacking the person's phone first and gaining access to it. After that, the hacker will try to obtain all the login credentials by tricking the person into logging into the Tesla app, which has been modified by the hacker. This is called a software hack. As a result, the hacker will be able to gain full access to the car using the information obtained and drive away with it.

In addition, the infotainment system of the car is also one of the vulnerabilities of Tesla. In a competition, a pair of hackers were able to hack and take control of the car by using its internet browser. Although the security measure for the car is installed in a way in which the location of the data is placed randomly, which makes it nearly impossible to hack Tesla yet, hackers were able to hack using a web browser bug. The hackers were able to gain access to the system and display a message of their own on the vehicle's IVI system. In another scenario, a group of hackers were able to hack into the web browser of the car and connect it to a modified Wi-Fi hotspot that is malicious. By doing this, they were able to unlock the car that was parked.

Another vulnerability that was discovered in Tesla is its navigation system while on Autopilot mode. This is done by spoofing an attack on the GPS navigation system. During Autopilot mode, the car is able to carry out functions such as steering, applying brake and accelerating by itself. At the same time, supervision of the driver is also required. Tesla can be hacked by using a few spoofing equipment in order to stage an attack on the car. Satellite coordinates that are fake will be sent to the car. This will cause the GPS receiver to receive the fake coordinates and carry out navigation based on that. Therefore, the hackers can control and choose to increase or decrease the speed of the car, change lanes or even stop it. This demonstrates that Tesla's security can be compromised by spoofing attacks.

These vulnerabilities may lead to serious impacts since the security of the car can be compromised. These are potential risks that can open doors for the occurrences of cyber-attacks. This is because the data of the owner will be exposed to hackers, and they can steal the data, especially financial information, since it is not well protected. This can even cause a ransomware attack on the owner of the vehicle in which he will have to pay the ransom amount demanded by the hacker. The owner will not be able to access the care system until the ransom is paid. Besides, the number of cases of car theft will also increase since hackers are able to hack the car within a few seconds and drive away with the car. Gaining access through the navigation system is also a potential risk because hackers will be operating the speed of the car, and it may cause confusion to the driver. The driver may tend to over speed assuming the car is moving too slow. This can be dangerous as it can cause car accidents and even risk the life of the driver.

3. METHODS OF ATTACKS

3.1. Key Fob

The role of a key fob is basically to function as a transmitter that commonly operates on a radio frequency that ranges about 315 MHz. RFID radio signals that are encrypted can be sent and received using the key fob. The range of the transmission signals varies according to the manufacturers of the vehicle, but generally, it is between 5 to 20 meters. Apart from that, there are antennas in the car which also are used for the transmission of radio signals that are encrypted. A relay attack can be carried out in the PKES system using the key fob because the vehicle can be unlocked by verification of just the signal that can communicate with the correct key within the proximity instead of verification of the correct key [4].

A key fob has to be near the car in order for the antenna of the vehicle to detect the signals from it and then unlock the vehicle automatically. Therefore, a hacker tends to use a radio amplification device that helps in boosting signals from the key fob, which is out of range or far from the vehicle. The device then intercepts and transmits the signal to another device which will be held by another hacker near the vehicle. This transmission of signals will then unlock the vehicle without even a key fob.

(Fig. **2**) illustrates a simple overview of the flow of a relay attack done using antennas and an amplifier. One antenna will be placed near the vehicle and another one near the key fob. A cable was used to connect the loops of both the antennas, which will then relay the low frequency or also known as LF signals, from them. An amplifier will then be placed between the antennas for the purpose of improving signal power. The loop of the antenna, which was placed near the handle of the vehicle, then captured the signals from it as a magnetic field. As a result, an alternating signal was created through induction due to the magnetic field. Next, the cable then received the signals and transmitted them over to the second antenna through the amplifier. The second antenna then created a current in it once the signal was received, which was then followed by the generation of a magnetic field within the proximity of the antenna. Then, the magnetic field started to demodulate the signal and later obtained the original message from the vehicle. It then caused the key to sending an authorisation message to start or open through the UHF or also known as the ultra-high frequency channel. The vehicle then sent a command to open it from the antenna outside to the key, as well as a command to start from the antenna inside. Therefore, the hacker initially had to place the relaying antenna near the handle of the vehicle for the key to send a signal to unlock the vehicle. Once this was done, the hackers then had to bring in the relaying antenna into the vehicle for it to send a message to the key to start the vehicle once the engine was started.

3.2. Attack *via* Tesla App in Android Smartphone

Each Tesla vehicle user has to install the Tesla app on their smartphones because it can be used for multiple reasons such as identifying the location of the vehicle, checking the remaining percentage of battery, charging status of the vehicle and many more. The owners of the vehicle have to install it on their Android or IOS phones. Researchers have found that there is a way to hack the car using the app on an Android smartphone. The lack of security of the app enables the vehicle owner to be exposed to a threat.

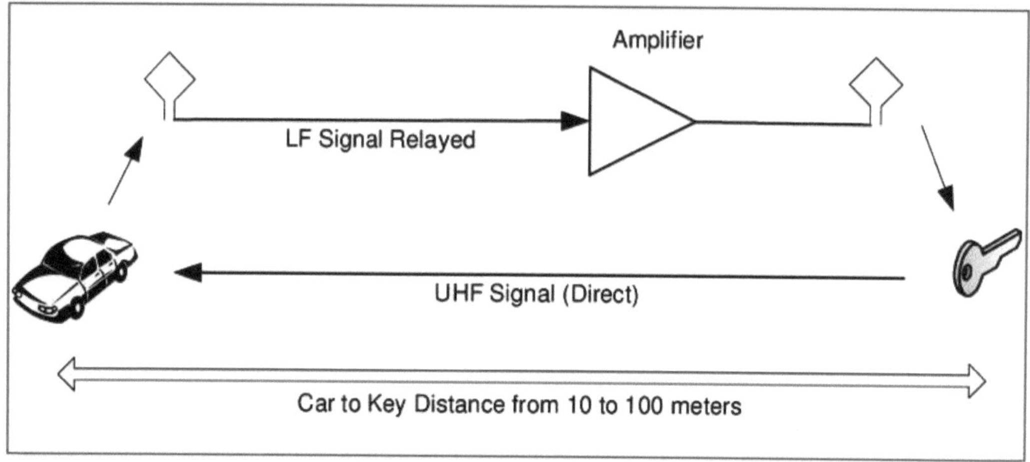

Fig. (2). Flow of relay attack [4].

This first step in carrying out this attack was to create an open Wi-Fi hotspot that can be accessed for free near a Tesla vehicle charging station as it particularly targets Tesla owners. The Wi-Fi hotspot was created with a name of a restaurant that was near the charging station. An advertisement was created to trick the owners into installing the malicious app in order to redeem free burgers in return at a restaurant nearby. The owner was redirected to the malware app in Google Play Store once he clicked the advertisement. This action is also known as a phishing attack. Malware will be installed on the phone once the owner installed the app. This malware then started to manipulate the Tesla app on the phone. Manipulation of the malware took place with escalation attack privilege, which is the same as using rooting apps. For instance, Kingroot and Towelroot are some examples of rooting apps. It can also be done by using malware such as HummingBad and Godless. The manipulation of the app was performed once the root permissions were obtained.

The hacker then started to search for the location of the OAuth token. This token was provided by the Tesla server to a Tesla companion app for the purpose of enabling the Tesla user to connect to this server for the first time with information such as username and password using the app. The tokens were usually stored in the sandbox folder of the app in the form of a file. Generally, the app will take the stored tokens from the file for any subsequent logins. Besides, the validity of the token was usually up to three months which indicated that the owner does not necessarily need to re-enter the login credentials always as it can remain valid for a period of up to ninety days.

The function of the malware was to locate this token and reset it. Without the token, the companion app showed an error when the owner wanted to log in and connect to the vehicle and asked to re-enter the information. The username and password will be sent to the hacker once the owner re-entered this information. This was because the malware from the app stored the information when the owner re-entered the username and password during the second attempt to log into the Tesla app. This enabled the hacker to track the exact location of the vehicle with the login credentials and OAuth token [6]. The hacker then proceeded to key in the username and password of the Tesla vehicle using his device once he got near the vehicle. As the vehicle has a keyless driving feature, the hacker then enabled the feature, which then allowed him to gain full access to the car and steal it easily. This attack took place due to a glitch in a phone app and not because of Tesla, but it gives the hacker an opportunity to exploit this vulnerability. In addition, it also portrayed that it is not safe to use third-party apps. Although this attack was made just for research purposes, it showcased the possibility of a hacker to exploit this vulnerability and gain control of the vehicle if this flaw was not rectified.

3.3. Attack *via* Infotainment System

A software bug is a security defect that is mainly used to gain access to a system that is not authorised which is usually done on a computer system. This bug can cause vulnerabilities in the security system to surface and to be exploited by hackers. Although the Tesla vehicle is made up of a complex software integration that has multiple functions, it can still be hacked by using a security bug. In a hacking competition, two hackers managed to hack the infotainment system of the vehicle. The hackers discovered a flaw in the system, which was a bug in the vehicle's browser. It was a JIT bug or also known as a just-in-time bug which was found in a component called renderer. Once the bug was discovered, the hackers were able to take control and exploit the interface of the web. Then, a webpage that was malicious was created and accessed from the display. As a result, the whole display screen got stuck, including the information that was shown too. This caused a denial of service or DoS to be uncovered. Apart from that, the hackers also gained entry and displayed their own message on the in-car web browser using the JIT bug.

3.4. GPS Spoofing Attack

Tesla vehicles also have a vulnerability in their navigation system. A group of researchers carried out a staged GPS spoofing attack on Tesla model 3. This spoofing attack was carried out when the Tesla vehicle was in Autopilot mode. The tools that were needed for the spoofing attack were GPS Spoofer, jammer and antenna. These tools can be obtained online at a very low cost. An antenna that was small was placed on the roof of the Tesla vehicle for the purpose of simulating an attack externally as well as for limiting the effect of it on the GPS receivers. The picture below illustrates the AutoPilot spoofing test. It shows the planned route that was supposed to be followed by the vehicle and also the actual car action towards a narrow pit stop.

The researchers travelled on the vehicle at a speed of 95 km/h, navigating in AutoPilot mode. The planned route was to travel along the highway and then make a major interchange at the exit of the highway. In order to trick the navigation system, fake satellite coordinates were transmitted by the researchers, who were then received by the GPS receiver. The fake satellite coordinates caused the vehicle to navigate based on it and trick it into thinking that the highway exit is 500 feet away, although, in reality, the exit is still about a mile away. This made the vehicle slow down rapidly and make an emergency turn off at a narrow pit stop. The vehicle driver managed to regain control of the vehicle because his hands were on the steering wheel throughout the process. However, the driver could not manoeuvre back to the highway lane because it was too late to make a turn and the whole scenario happened quickly. The lanes taken by the vehicle while in Autopilot mode were based on the data from Google Map and GPS. The researchers also could spoof the data and cause the vehicle to accelerate and decelerate fast and change lanes based on the manipulated data that may lead to extreme instability while driving. The range for spoofing is limited with the use of an antenna. An amplifier can be used to extend the range for spoofing vehicles. This GPS spoof was carried out within a minute.

Another threat that was found due to the impact of GPS spoofing was it affected the air suspension system. The air suspension system of the vehicle is linked to the navigation system. Therefore, it caused the height of the car to change unexpectedly while the vehicle was moving. This was because the vehicle thought it was driving on multiple locations with different road surfaces. Generally, the vehicle would be lowered on smooth road surfaces while elevating the vehicle's undercarriage when on roads with rough surfaces for the purpose of greater aerodynamics—this help in avoiding any obstacles while driving. The impact of this attack is dangerous because it can cause danger to the driver as well as other drivers too, and this makes it a crime to attack the GPS system of any vehicle [7].

4. METHODS OF DEFENSE

4.1. Key Fob Hack

There are a few methods of defence that can be used as countermeasures against relay attacks. One of the methods is shielding the key. Communication between the vehicle and the key fob should be prevented except for a situation when the owner wants to use the vehicle. A protective layer of the metallic shield can be placed around the key fob in order to create a Faraday cage surrounding the key in the case. No signals can be received by the key while in the case, and the owner has to get the key from the case to unlock and start the vehicle. The next measure is to come up with a modification to the software. A simple modification on the software should be done to enable users to disable the PKES system of the vehicle temporarily if they want to. By doing this, the vehicle would only be able to unlock and start if the owner uses the key fob to press the open button since the passive entry is not activated. This is an effective measure for users, especially when parking the vehicle in places that are not safe such as underground parking. Another measure would be embedding radio frequency distance bounding with the PKES system. There are two entities: the verifier and the prover. They are a group of protocols in which the verifier has to measure the upper bound distance between these two entities. This is known as distance bounding. Messages that are exchanged rapidly between the prover and the verifier are used for the purpose of obtaining distance bound. The initial step is the prover will receive a challenge from the verifier and has to reply after processing it. The time taken to send and receive the reply, excluding the processing time, is measured, and the distance bound between entities of both the devices are computed. The challenges from the verifier vary and are not easy to be predicted. If the time to respond to the challenge gets delayed or if the distance between both the verifier and prover are not constant, then the system would be able to deduce that this entry is not reliable and would require the owner to press the open button to unlock the car. This measure helps as a defence against relay attacks since it helps in measuring the accurate distance between both devices [8].

4.2. Tesla App

Hackers were able to gain access to the car and drive away with it due to the lack of security in the smartphone. One way to combat this issue is to avoid using free Wi-Fi at public places since not all free Wi-Fi is safe, and hackers can use it as a channel to gain access to a person's smartphone and obtain their personal information and credentials. Users also should always upgrade their smartphone system if there are any software updates, especially Android phones. This is because Android smartphones with versions older than Lollipop 5.1 are vulnerable to this attack. Next, the OAuth tokens stored in the sandbox folder of the app in the form of a file should be encrypted instead of in the form of plain text. This is to ensure that hackers will not be able to exploit it.

4.3. Infotainment System

A software bug can cause vulnerabilities in the security system to surface and to be exploited by hackers. Over-the-air (OTA) feature in Tesla is used for the purpose of updating the vehicle if there is an issue. This feature can be used by all Tesla owners to immediately make a software bug report to the company without much hassle. An immediate bug report can be sent to Tesla by using the voice recognition system of the vehicle. Once the system gets recognition, the owner can send a brief message explaining the big issue that is faced. Once the report is completed, the infotainment system of the vehicle will take a screenshot of the report. The owner will then be requested to submit a picture and voice message of the owner to Tesla together with the report. Once the report is sent to Tesla, the issue will be fixed by sending a software update to the vehicle by using the OTA feature.

4.4. GPS Spoof

There are a few safety measures that can be taken to avoid attacks related to GPS spoofing. Firstly, manufacturers of the vehicle should come up with a design in which the position of the antenna should be placed in a way the vehicle would not take ground-based signals easily. An obscure antenna should be placed in a part of the vehicle which is not easily visible to others. Therefore, it would not be easy for hackers to manipulate the navigation system of the vehicle. Further safeguards step can be taken by Tesla manufacturers by adding barriers for the purpose of hiding the location of the antenna. This can be done by placing plastic fencing surrounding it, which acts as a barrier that, at the same time, does not interfere with the signals. Decoy antennas also can be placed further from the real antennas. This is to ensure that the legitimate signals would not be manipulated due to spoofing attacks. Next, blocking antennas can also be included in the design of the vehicle because they help against any signal interference and jamming. Apart from that, additional sensors can be added to the vehicle for the purpose of identifying and detecting signals that are spoofed. The signals then can be sent to the monitoring team of Tesla to identify and alert the owner. Finally, the GPS receiver should be further upgraded in order to be able to detect and differentiate the spoofed and original satellite signals. Once the receiver discovers and flags it as a spoof, it should exclude the fake coordinates from the positioning calculation.

5. CONCEPTUAL FRAMEWORK

Tesla is one of the highly computerised vehicles in the automotive industry. The security of the vehicle can be further increased for a more efficient and safer driving experience. This can be done by coming up with four layers of security for the vehicle combined with the existing vehicle security system for further protection. The purpose of the protection is to ensure interfaces that are responsible for connecting the vehicle to the outer world, domain isolations that are provided by the gateways and the features of the vehicle that are implemented by the processing units are secured.

The conceptual framework (Fig. **3**) shows four layers of protection that should be added to the security defense of Tesla vehicles [8]. The first layer is security interfaces. Most vehicle networks are not well-protected, and a hacker can take control of a vehicle once they gain access to the telematics control unit (TCU). The purpose of this layer is to add secure elements such as microcontrollers to the TCU to achieve maximum security.

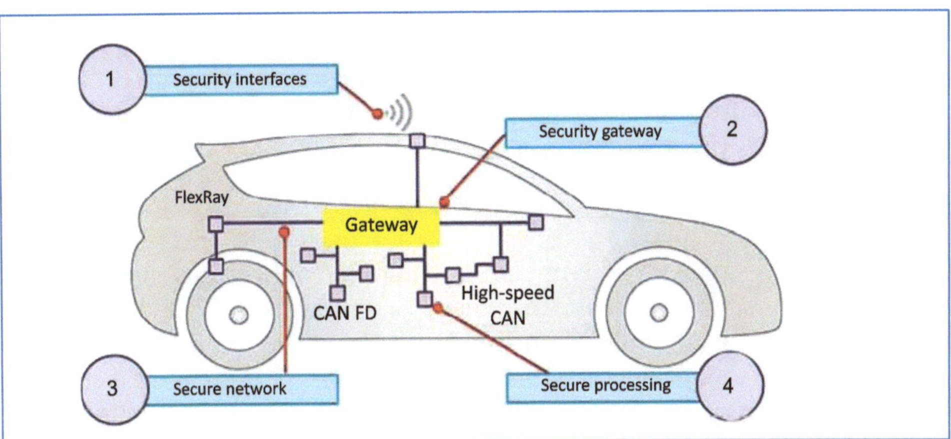

Fig. (3). Conceptual framework on further improvement of tesla security [8].

The second layer is made up of a security gateway. Lack of security in the gateway results in hackers gaining access to the vehicle in which the vehicle was hacked through the network and was able to send a message. Therefore, it is fundamental to improve the security of the gateway. On-board diagnostics (OBD) and TCU can separate the central gateway ECU from the network. Then it proceeds to break up the network of the vehicle, followed by deciding which nodes communicate with the rest of the other nodes. It will be decided by the gateway firewall. This firewall is the primary function of the gateway for separating the outer interfaces from the critical inner networks.

The third layer is a secure network. Although the surface of attack of the vehicle's architecture is decreased due to the split of domains in the network, the vehicle is still vulnerable to attack because of the sub-domains. Therefore, the purpose of the third layer is to protect these sub-domains from attack. The protection for the sub-domains is done by adding four safeguards which are authentication of the message, encryption, intrusion detection and validation of the level of ECU. Firstly, the authentication of the message is included with a cryptographic code. The role of this code is to ensure that the sender is authentic and the received message will not be altered. Next is encryption, in which the messages between the ECUs will be encrypted. The third step is intrusion detection for detecting and blocking malicious packets by using the recognition of patterns. This step will be done before the malicious packets reach the microcontroller. The last step is the validation of the ECU level, in which regular verification will be done on the authenticity of the ECUs.

The last layer is secure processing which plays a role in ensuring if the software of the processor is genuine. An authentic image code can be guaranteed by modern microcontrollers equipped with a secure boot. In addition, a mechanism for software upgrade is necessary because the vehicle is made up of a complex system, and there are chances that vulnerabilities are discovered. In such a situation where a software bug is discovered, the OEMs should be able to respond fast and update the software of the vehicle securely.

CONCLUSION

IoT is basically a concept of embedding internet connectivity and computing capabilities on most objects. There are many examples of IoT devices in various industries. Tesla is an example of an IoT device from the automotive industry. It is built with many unique features that make it different compared to the rest of the vehicles in the same industry. Although it is one of the safest vehicles in the world, it also has a few vulnerabilities that allow hackers to exploit and gain access to the vehicle. Some of the vulnerabilities that can be found are in the key system, Tesla application in smartphones, the infotainment as well as the navigation system of the vehicle. Hackers can exploit any of these vulnerabilities and take control of the car within a short period of time. Manufacturers of Tesla should come up with necessary steps to fix these issues and prevent the vehicle from being hacked. The lack of security in the system of the vehicle should be addressed, and further steps should be taken to increase the security of the vehicle. This can be done by adding four layers of security to the existing security of the vehicle. The four layers are security interfaces, security gateway, secure network and secure processing.

REFERENCES

[1] M.A. Eltayeb, "The Internet of Things", *Int. J. Hyperconnectivity and the Internet of Things,* vol. 2, no. 1, pp. 1-11, 2018. [http://dx.doi.org/10.4018/IJHIoT.2018010101]

[2] S. Szymkowski, "Tesla Begins To Observe In-Car Data Usage, Likely As Free Connectivity Ends", *CNET, Sept.* 25, 2019. [Online]. Available at: https://www.cnet.com/roadshow/ news/ tesla-data-connectivity- internet-wifi/ [Accessed 22 October 2020].

[3] M. Mangram, "The globalisation of Tesla Motors: a strategic marketing plan analysis", *J. Strategic Marketing*, vol. 20, issue 4, pp. 1-24, January 2012. [Online]. Available from: https://www.tandfonline.com/doi/abs/10.1080/0965254X.2012.657224 [Accessed 18th October 2020].

[4] J. Li, Y. Dong, S. Fang, H. Zhang, and D. Xu, "User context detection for relay attack resistance in passive keyless entry and start system", *Sensors,* vol. 20, no. 16, p. 4446, 2020. [http://dx.doi.org/10.3390/s20164446] [PMID: 32784905]

[5] A. Grau, How To Stop Automotive Key-Fob Encryption Hacks, "electronicdesign.com, 2 May 2020. [Online]". Available: https: //www.electronicdesign.com/markets/automotive/article/21130290/how-to- stop- automotive- keyfob- encryption- hacks

[6] "Researchers Hack Into Tesla Car Using An Android App," November 24, 2016. [Online]. Available: https://cyware.com/news/researchers-hack-into-tesla-car-using-an-android-app-85fa582d

[7] M. Gauthier, "Researchers Target Tesla Model 3 In Spoofing Attack, Get It To Turn Off The Highway 2020. Researchers Target Tesla Model 3 In Spoofing Attack, Get It To Turn Off The Highway", carscoops.com, 24 June 2019. [Online]. Available: https://www.carscoops.com/2019/06/researchers-target-tesla-model-3-in-spoofing-attack-get-it-to-turn-off-the-highway [Accessed 27 October 2020].

[8] A. Birnie, and T.V. Roermund, "4 Layers of Automotive Security", 26th August 26 [Online]. http: //electronicdesign.com /print/ automotive/4- layers- automotive- security [Accessed 29 October 2020].

CHAPTER 3

Malware Analysis and Malicious Activity Detection using Machine Learning

Muhammad Jawed Chowdhury[1], **Julia Juremi**[2,*] and **Maryam Var Naseri**[1]

[1] *School of Computing & Technology, Asia Pacific University of Technology and Innovation, Kuala Lumpur, Malaysia*

[2] *Forensic and Cyber Security Research Center, Asia Pacific University of Technology and Innovation, Kuala Lumpur, Malaysia*

Abstract: Criminals are working day and night to get hold of the data. They are also getting more intelligent and are also using AI-powered threats to exploit vulnerabilities to perform an attack. Information security is at a higher risk, now more than ever. Due to the popularity of internet usage by users, the IT infrastructure is prone to security threats. The damage done by computer malware and viruses is known to cost billions of US dollars. Hence, this paper reviews the ways of integrating technology such as machine learning, neural networks, deep learning, *etc*. which can help to develop an intelligent system to protect and prevent the IT infrastructure from security threats. The authors proposed AIVA, a Machine learning (ML) based detection system which is able to classify a suspicious object as "safe" or "dangerous". AIVA is composed of three core components: static analysis, machine learning, and malicious detection.

Keywords: Confusion matrix, Machine learning, Malware analysis, Portable executable (PE) file.

1. INTRODUCTION

Due to the high usage of the internet, it is prone to security threats. Therefore, we need intelligent solutions such as Artificial Intelligence (AI) to combat security threats [1]. A study defines AI as an advanced algorithm that mimics traditional human abilities such as problem-solving and learning from its experiences. As artificial intelligence becomes more powerful, we can use it in the field of cybersecurity to detect security threats such as malware, *etc*.

* **Corresponding author Julia Juremi:** Forensic and Cyber Security Research Center, Asia Pacific University of Technology and Innovation, Kuala Lumpur, Malaysia; E-mail: Julia.juremi@apu.edu.my

Muhammad Ehsan Rana & Manoj Jayabalan (Eds.)

To implement the various techniques of artificial intelligence to detect security threats, we must also discuss the evolution of security threats such as malware, viruses, *etc*. Malware and virus can spread quickly due to the presence of ever-increasing use of networks and the internet. According to a study done by FireEye [2], 47% of the organizations have faced malware incidents [3]. Another study proposed technological solutions that can be added to increase the effectiveness and performance of malware detection. These solutions include cloud computing, network-based detection systems, web, virtual machines, and hybrid methods and technologies [4]. A study states that traditional defense systems use signature-based techniques. These techniques are unable to detect malware.

The purpose of malware analysis is to provide a deeper understanding of several aspects, such as malware behaviour and its evolution. It can analyse the malicious code in the malware and understand its risks and true intentions. It can also capture the properties that can be used to improve security measures and make it difficult to avoid detection [6]. Hence the author supports the process of using machine learning to extract features from Windows executable. Among various platforms such as Android, MacOS, *etc*., Windows Operating System remains the preferred target among the rest due to its popularity.

As illustrated in Fig. (**1**), malware analysis by using machine learning can be divided into three major categories. The first category defines the objectives of the analysis, the second describes the features that the malware analysis is based on and finally the third one being what type of machine learning algorithm is used.

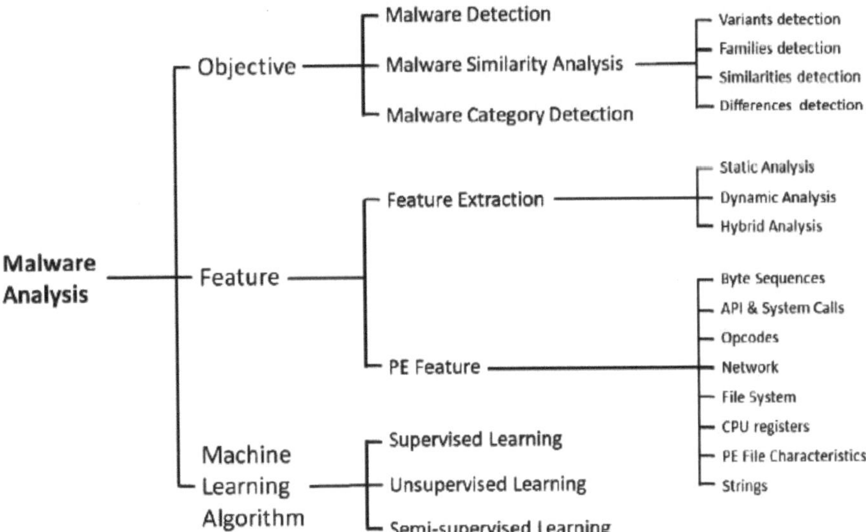

Fig. (1). Taxonomy of malware analysis.

The objective of analysing malware is to detect whether a given file is malicious. From the findings, the author emphasizes the importance of knowing whether a file is malicious in advance as it allows it to get blocked before the malware becomes harmful. The second objective is to spot the similarities among malware, to help understand how new malwares are evolving and how they differ from the previous malware. The analysis of the malware can be derived by detecting their variants, families, similarities, and differences. Attackers often reuse the available codes and resources from previous malware samples to develop variants. By recognizing malware as a variant, it helps to understand how the variant has evolved from its predecessor. By knowing the similarities, it helps to narrow down the search more towards the features that have not been discovered before. Analysing the differences can give us new information to look forward to for new insights. The authors [5] mention categorizing the malware according to their malicious behaviour as it helps to describe the malware. For example, if the malware is encrypting and asking for a ransom, it can be classified as "Ransomware".

Detection systems that are developed with malware analysis can decide if an object is a threat based on the data that the system has collected. This data may be collected at different phases: Pre-execution phase and Post-execution phase. The pre-execution phase is basically static analysis which is knowing anything about the file without its execution whereas post-execution is basically dynamic analysis which is analysing the file and recording its behaviour and activity during its execution process.

Feature extraction is the process of identifying the key features in a Portable Executable (PE) file and extracting the features [6]. For the machine learning algorithm, we need to consider what features to analyse, how to extract these features from a Portable Executable (PE) file by using static, dynamic or hybrid analysis. Static analysis is performed before the malware is executed. It analyses what its true intentions are and what code it is trying to execute. Dynamic analysis, on the other hand, is performed after the malware has already been executed, analysing its functionality. This is mostly carried out in a safe environment such as the Sandboxes [7]. A study mentions some of the examples of information that can be extracted by dynamic analysis. They include API calls, system calls, instruction traces, registry changes, memory writes, *etc*. Moreover, hybrid analysis is a combination of both static and dynamic analysis. It merges two aspects of analysis which are signature specifications of malware code and then combines it with malware behavioural parameters. Due to this approach, hybrid analysis overcomes the limitation of merging these two aspects of static and dynamic analysis [8].

The Portable Executable (PE) is a file format for executables that contain lots of information and features that are found to be important. Machine Learning tools and techniques can be used to extract these important features from malicious PE files and then to create models that can distinguish between benign and malicious files. In addition, machine learning can automatically extract the importance of these features as well as the dependencies between them. The PE file format provides detailed information on the true nature and purpose of the PE file. Malware creators use the said file format to create malware and target Windows users as it is the most used operating system worldwide. A PE file structure consists of two sections, a header, and a section. Fig. (**2**) is a graphical illustration of a typical PE file structure. The header contains details about the executable and the sections contain the code and the data for the executable. The PE header contains the information the Operating System (OS) required in order to run the executable. The information can tell us about the functionality of the malware and how the malware interacts with the OS.

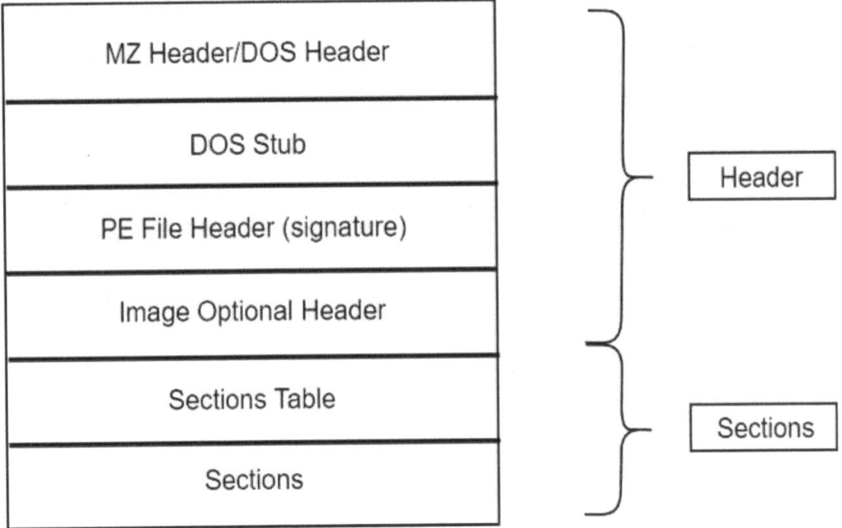

Fig. (2). A typical structure of a Portable Executable.

PE Sections Structure separates the different logical and physical parts of the program. The section table immediately follows the optional header. Sections can include binary code, strings, configuration, pictures, and more. In addition to containing both the code and the data that the programmer codes, it also contains instructions on how to load the executable into memory and where the sections are located. It can contain several sections which contain the code and data used by the executable. Table (**1**) shows some of the commonly used sections and their functions in an executable.

Table 1. Sections and its functions.

Section Name	Function
.code / .text	Executable code
.data	Stores data (R/W)
.rdata	Stores data (Read Only)
.idata	Stores the Import Table
.edata	Stores Export Data
.rsrc	Stores Resources (String, icons)

The sections in a malware executable can differ when compared to a typical executable. This can happen due to several factors including the compiler which is used to generate the PE. As stated before, malware developers often encrypt the code to avoid detection. This is accomplished by using a custom compiler which enables them to do the following operations: packing, encryption, manipulation of strings, obfuscation, anti-debugging features, stripping of identifying information, *etc* [9]. Table (**2**) shows some of the names of the sections that are linked with known compilers, builders, and packing infrastructure.

Table 2. Compilers, builders and packing infrastructure.

Section Name	Builders/Compilers/Packing Infrastructure
Mpres	Mpres Packer
Upx	UPX
Tsuarch	TSULoader
Petite	Petit packer
Rmnet	Ramnit Packer
Vmp	VMProtect

2. AIVA SYSTEM ARCHITECTURE

AIVA is a tool developed with python for the Windows operating system in order to fulfill the aims and objectives of the researcher. Firstly, to be able to analyse a Portable Executable (PE) file and extract a selected number of interesting features, and secondly, to train a model with a dataset that includes the distinguishable features of both benign and malware files in order to classify the files in the dataset. Finally, AIVA is developed to be able to detect a malicious file with the integration of VirusTotal Application Programming Interface (API).

The AIVA tool as illustrated in Fig. (**3**) is composed of three core components; static analysis, machine learning, and malicious detection. In the process of static analysis, any PE file can be analysed, and its interesting features can be extracted and exported into a CSV file. In the next component, a model can be trained with different types of machine learning algorithms using 70% of the dataset consisting the distinguishable features. After the training phase, the model will then enter the testing phase where it is tested using the other 30% of the dataset. The results produced from the testing phase are then evaluated using classification metrics. The final component enables the user to upload any file to the VirusTotal API and scan for maliciousness as well as view the results returned from the API. The following section discusses the three core components and their features in-depth.

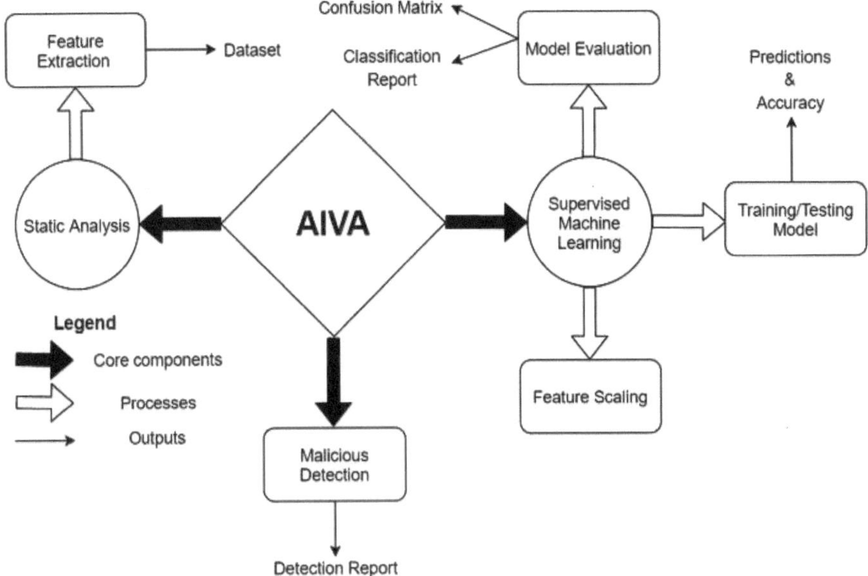

Fig. (3). AIVA model.

2.1. AIVA Core Components

2.1.1. Static Analysis

Static analysis is performed where the malware isn't executed yet. This is where the user can analyse any PE file after entering the file directory. This component consists of several features. One of them displays all the information about the PE file and allows the user to analyse the entire PE file structure. With this feature, the user is able to inspect headers, analyse sections' data, retrieve embedded data, *etc*. Another feature of the AIVA tool allows the user to inspect a file and extract a selected number of interesting features which can then be exported to a CSV file. This CSV file can later be used to feed the machine learning algorithm in order to train the model.

2.1.2. Supervised Machine Learning

This core component is concerned with training a model under supervised machine learning with various types of machine learning algorithms. The main objective of this core component is to find out if the machine learning model is able to recognize and memorize patterns according to the input provided. In supervised machine learning, the algorithm learns from the training dataset provided. This training dataset has labelled data and the correct answers based on which the model makes predictions and corrects itself until it reaches peak performance [10]. Moreover, the dataset also contains various interesting features of the PE file. This component also consists of several features and steps that are needed in order to train a model successfully.

2.1.3. VirusTotal Application Programming Interface (API)

VirusTotal Application Programming Interface (API) VirusTotal on [11] is a website that aggregates over 70 antivirus scanners made by Symantec, Kaspersky, F-secure, *etc*., and URL/domain blacklisting services. The site allows any user to upload a suspicious file, to find out if any of the antivirus scanners flag it as malicious. The site also provides detailed results on the uploaded file, as well as real-time updates. One of the services provided by VirusTotal is the public API that allows users to automate scripts in order to upload and scan files or URLs without using the website interface. The VirusTotal public API is another component that the AIVA tool incorporates. This component enables users to find out whether a suspicious file is malicious or not upon entering the directory of the suspicious file.

3. RESULTS AND DISCUSSIONS

In the process of developing the tool, all the components and features discussed are integrated to ensure the system is operational. Fig. (**4**) displays the main menu screen of the AIVA tool which is divided into three sections: static analysis, supervised machine learning, and malicious file detection. The main menu consists of the primary features that are available to the user. The user can enter the appropriate digit that is assigned to the list of available features.

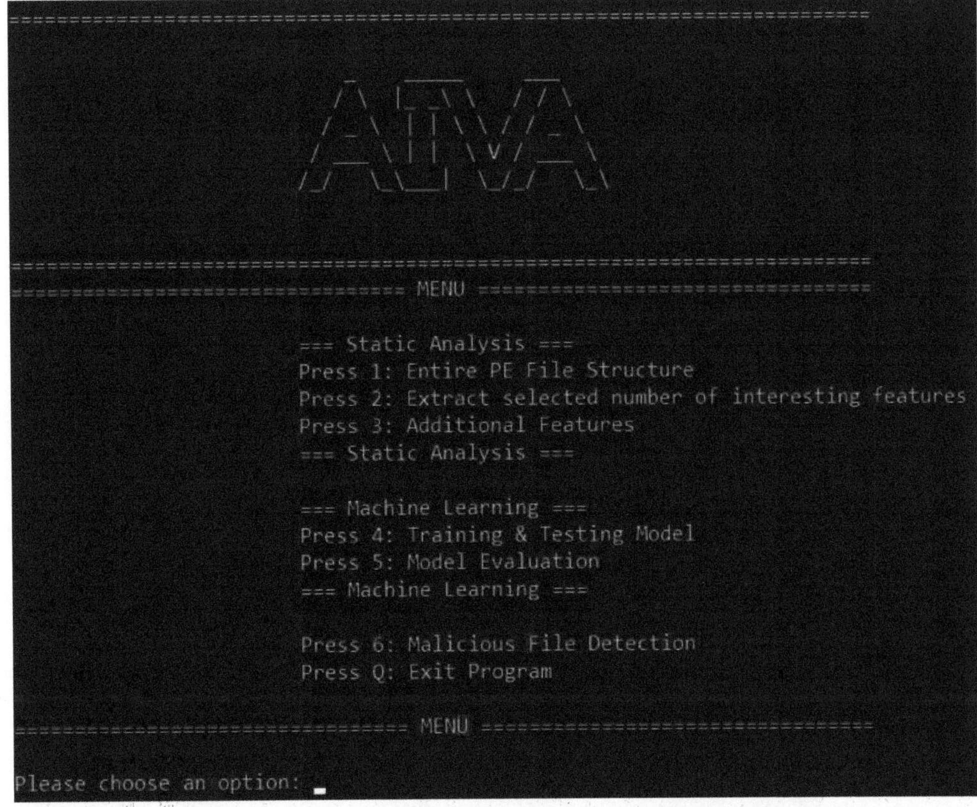

Fig. (4). AIVA main menu.

One of the options available allows the user to examine the data in any PE file structure. The user will need to enter a valid directory to the PE file. The following Fig. (**5**) shows a part of the result which displays the PE file's FILE_HEADER and OPTIONAL_HEADER.

The algorithms that were used to train the model will be evaluated using two evaluation metrics. Classification report and Confusion matrix. Fig. (**6**) shows the accuracy of the two machine learning algorithms and their classification report, while Fig. (**7**) shows the confusion matrix where the table compares the actual values with the predicted values using the machine learning model.

The following Fig. (**8**) displays the results from VirusTotal API once a file has been scanned. A total of 63 anti-virus scanners have detected the EICAR Test file.

```
----------PE Sections----------

[IMAGE_SECTION_HEADER]
0x228      0x0   Name:                       .text
0x230      0x8   Misc:                       0xE866D0
0x230      0x8   Misc_PhysicalAddress:       0xE866D0
0x230      0x8   Misc_VirtualSize:           0xE866D0
0x234      0xC   VirtualAddress:             0x1000
0x238      0x10  SizeOfRawData:              0xE86800
0x23C      0x14  PointerToRawData:           0x400
0x240      0x18  PointerToRelocations:       0x0
0x244      0x1C  PointerToLinenumbers:       0x0
0x248      0x20  NumberOfRelocations:        0x0
0x24A      0x22  NumberOfLinenumbers:        0x0
0x24C      0x24  Characteristics:            0x60000020
Flags: IMAGE_SCN_CNT_CODE, IMAGE_SCN_MEM_EXECUTE, IMAGE_SCN_MEM_READ
Entropy: 6.556491 (Min=0.0, Max=8.0)
MD5     hash: 293e4aeed4f38d85c63f61793a194947
SHA-1   hash: d49b273d1150dc2ea4b51294b3c06e800729633a
SHA-256 hash: f2e52a2728e2a351854c5e95bfb3d2c55711e936429c310972faed9a
SHA-512 hash: 447a9890471ac87d6c313f0e7ee5eccfe9c584da3fed6d297143b7b
5876fd6ad293bf8a7b3ea8

[IMAGE_SECTION_HEADER]
0x250      0x0   Name:                       .rdata
0x258      0x8   Misc:                       0x233314
0x258      0x8   Misc_PhysicalAddress:       0x233314
0x258      0x8   Misc_VirtualSize:           0x233314
```

Fig. (5). PE file structure data.

```
Naive-Bayes accuracy: 36.00%

              precision    recall  f1-score   support

           0       0.28      0.99      0.44      1476
           1       0.98      0.15      0.26      4408

    accuracy                           0.36      5884
   macro avg       0.63      0.57      0.35      5884
weighted avg       0.81      0.36      0.30      5884

LinearSVC accuracy: 96.40%

              precision    recall  f1-score   support

           0       0.93      0.93      0.93      1476
           1       0.98      0.98      0.98      4408

    accuracy                           0.96      5884
   macro avg       0.95      0.95      0.95      5884
weighted avg       0.96      0.96      0.96      5884
```

Fig. (6). AIVA classification report.

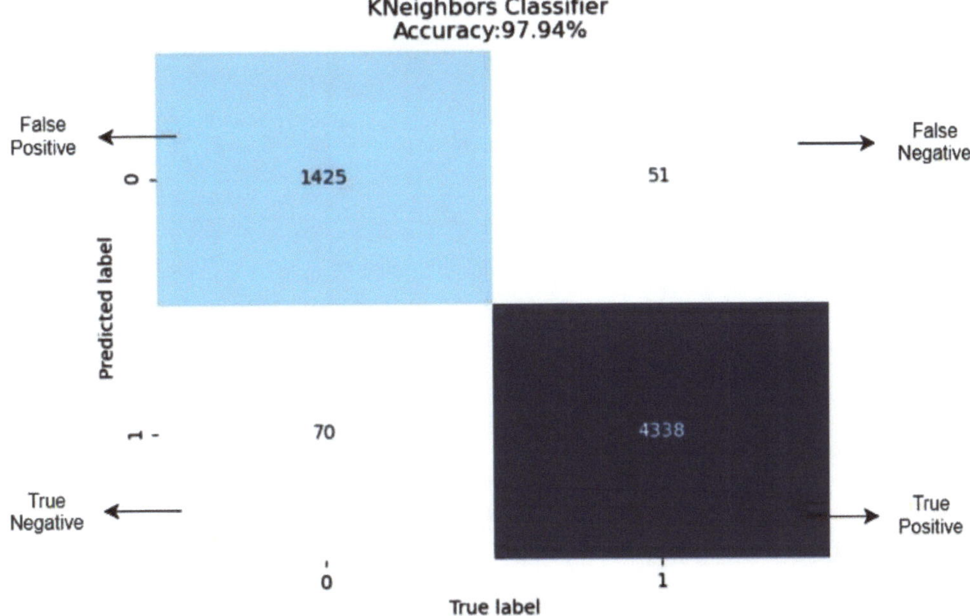

Fig. (7). AIVA confusion matrix.

```
File detected as Malicious in VirusTotal database!
Detected by number of Antivirus engines: 63
VirusTotal Report:  https://www.virustotal.com/gui/file/275a021bbfb6489e54d47189
9f7db9d1663fc695ec2fe2a2c4538aabf651fd0f/detection/f-275a021bbfb6489e54d471899f7
db9d1663fc695ec2fe2a2c4538aabf651fd0f-1597501166

                    *****Anti-virus scanners*****

                       detected              version  \
Bkav                       True           1.3.0.9899
Elastic                    True                4.0.6
MicroWorld-eScan           True           14.0.409.0
FireEye                    True            32.36.1.0
CAT-QuickHeal              True                14.00
ALYac                      True              1.1.1.5
Malwarebytes              False            3.6.4.335
Zillya                     True           2.0.0.4155
SUPERAntiSpyware           True           5.6.0.1032
Sangfor                    True                  1.0
K7AntiVirus                True         11.130.35004
Alibaba                    True              0.3.0.5
K7GW                       True         11.130.35004
Baidu                      True              1.0.0.2
F-Prot                     True            4.7.1.166
SymantecMobileInsight      True                  2.0
Symantec                   True             1.11.0.0
TotalDefense               True            37.1.62.1
APEX                       True                 6.59
```

Fig. (8). AIVA integrated virustotal API report.

The authors have also validated the malicious detection component of the AIVA tool. The following Fig. (**9**) shows the results from VirusTotal web interface by scanning the EICAR test file.

Fig. (9). Virus total api web interface.

CONCLUSION

The research outlines the capabilities and possibilities of using Artificial Intelligence (AI). AI's ability to automatically learn and improve from experiences makes it more robust as a detection system. With the help of one of its components which is machine learning, it is able to self-learn and maximize performance. With AIVA, the researcher was able to demonstrate the application of machine learning with static analysis to classify malware and achieve high accuracy. As for malicious detection, AIVA is able to scan a file and generate a report based on the findings from the VirusTotal. After the development phase, the AIVA tool is then tested by users to get their feedback. Based on that feedback, changes are made accordingly regarding the source code design, Command Line Interface design, and the components.

REFERENCES

[1] Avira Download Security Software For Windows, Mac, Android & Ios | Avira Antivirus, 2020. [Online] Available: https://www.avira.com/ [Accessed: 8th Feb. 2020].

[2] J. Brownlee, "Machine learning mastery with python", *Machine Learning Mastery Pty Ltd,* vol. 527, pp. 100-120, 2016.

[3] A. Damodaran, F.D. Troia, C.A. Visaggio, T.H. Austin, and M. Stamp, "A comparison of static, dynamic, and hybrid analysis for malware detection", *J. Comput. Virol. Hacking Tech.,* vol. 13, no. 1, pp. 1-12, 2017.
[http://dx.doi.org/10.1007/s11416-015-0261-z]

[4] "DeepAI, Feature Extraction", 2020. [Online] Available: https://deepai.org/machine-learning-glossa-y-and-terms/feature-extraction [Accessed: 11 Feb. 2020].

[5] "LEVIATHAN: Command and Control Communications on Planet Earth Black Hat Las Vegas", Available: https://www.fireeye.com/content/dam/fireeye-www/global/en/current-threats/pdfs/r-

t-leviathan.pdf May 2019.

[6] K. Mathur, and S. Hiranwal, "A Survey on Techniques in Detection and Analyzing Malware Executables", *Int. J. Adv. Res. Comput. Sci. Softw. Eng.,* vol. 3, no. 4, pp. 422-428, 2013. Corpus ID: 45091414

[7] I.A. Saeed, A. Selamat, and A.M. Abuagoub, "A Survey on Malware and Malware Detection Systems", *Int. J. Comput. Appl.,* vol. 67, no. 16, 2016. [http://dx.doi.org/10.5120/11480-7108]

[8] "Cyberbit, 5 Open Source Malware Tools You Should Have in Your Arsenal" 2016. [Online]. Available: https://www.cyberbit.com/blog/endpoint-security/open-source-malware-analysis-tools/ [Accessed: 4th Jan 2019].

[9] E. Gandotra, D. Bansal, and S. Sofat, "Malware analysis and classification: A survey", *J. Inform. Sec.,* 2014. [http://dx.doi.org/10.4236/jis.2014.52006]

[10] D. Ucci, L. Aniello, and R. Baldoni, "Survey of machine learning techniques for malware analysis", *Comput. Secur.,* vol. 81, pp. 123-147, 2019. [http://dx.doi.org/10.1016/j.cose.2018.11.001]

[11] Virustotal, [Online]. Available: https://www.virustotal.com/ [Accessed: 4th Jan 2019].

CHAPTER 4

Secure IoT based Home Automation by Identifying Vulnerabilities and Threats

Abdullah Khalid[1], **Nor Azlina Abdul Rahman**[2] and **Khalida Shajaratuddur Harun**[1,*]

[1] *School of Computing & Technology, Asia Pacific University of Technology and Innovation, Kuala Lumpur, Malaysia*

[2] *Forensic and Cyber Security Research Center, Asia Pacific University of Technology and Innovation, Kuala Lumpur, Malaysia*

Abstract: The Internet of Things (IoT) is a mesh network of “electronic things” that are capable of acquiring data using embedded sensors and customized software or technologies, amalgamating and exchanging the information with other devices, as well as executing a customized action. This encompasses everything connected to the internet from the smallest devices such as coffee makers to sophisticated industrial control systems. As the IoT aggressively becomes interwoven in every aspect of our lives, cyber-security has become a necessity. This research aims to highlight the security vulnerabilities in IoT-based Home Automation, discuss the risks that end users can be faced with, as well as provide defense against the classified risks.

Keywords: Business continuity planning, Home automation, Internet of things, Smart home, Smart home security, Smart home vulnerabilities.

1. INTRODUCTION

The term “Internet of Things” was coined by Kevin Ashton back in the 1990s, where his idea was simply to install an RFID tag, a tiny microchip, in everything that his company produced [1]. The recent aggressive boom in the production of IoT and its applications has not only made a huge impact on people’s daily lives but also on businesses. The world of IoT is presently gigantic, according to Priceonomics [2], there are currently 50 billion IoT devices, which will generate 4 zettabytes of data as of 2020. The yearly sales revenue from IoT devices is forecasted to hit $1.6 trillion by 2025 from just $200 billion today. This will make you to be able to conserve more energy as well as be less worried about the security of your home since all of the installed devices can be accessed remotely

* **Corresponding author Khalida Shajaratuddur Harun:** School of Computing & Technology, Asia Pacific University of Technology and Innovation, Kuala Lumpur, Malaysia; E-mail: khalida@staffemail.apu.edu.my

Muhammad Ehsan Rana & Manoj Jayabalan (Eds.)

from anywhere. Lastly, the Smart home architecture is completely scalable, providing homeowners the feasibility of upgrading their existing appliances or adding new ones to the existing network which remain updated to the latest technology trends [3].

2. SMART HOME IOT

The enormous diffusion of various devices connected to each other in the number of billions has created the serious necessity of implementing robust security measures, as all these devices are continuously connected to the internet in one way or another. The convenience of controlling your home lights and garage doors just with a few taps on your smartphone is becoming a habit for many people, thus making the smart home industry worth billions of dollars. It was expected that by the end of 2019, the smart home devices sold would add up to a whopping 1.9 billion. Furthermore, it is predicted that the smart home market could grow to $53 billion by the year 2022 [4].

As shown in (Fig. **1**), the market shares of various IoT sectors, it can be seen that smart home automation holds the four largest market shares from all the IoT sectors.

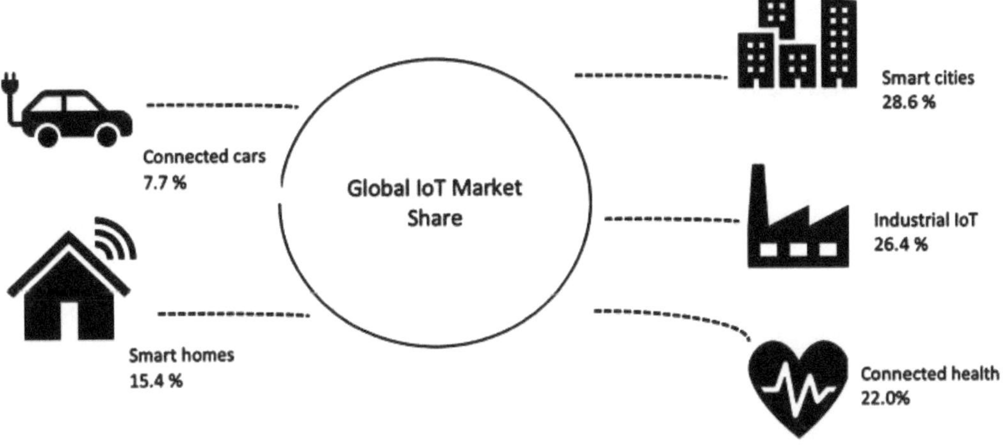

Fig. (1). Global IoT market share [4].

Due to the low-cost availability of most of these devices, the manufacturers do not spend an ample amount of time or effort in properly securing them and continuously improving towards the betterment of their security. These devices have ended up, in turn, being an attractive choice of targets for cyber-criminals [5]. There is a rapid increase in the number of threats, with the attacks increasing both in sophistication and in number. Alongside the increase in the number of attackers, the tools they are utilizing have become more efficient and effective than before. The larger the number of connected devices, the greater the attack surface they provide for cyber-criminals. Not all IoT devices having vulnerabilities are considered insecure, however, in many cases, they can only be exploited by physical access to the device itself. This will result in there being a lesser risk for the average end-user. Yet again there are many ways the devices can be penetrated remotely through the internet, and be abused with malicious intentions [6]. It is crucial to identify the vulnerabilities that currently and potentially exist, along with finding out what the impact exploiting these could have on the end-user.

2.1. Smart Homes Architecture

The primary goal of smart home architecture is to connect all IoT devices and achieve access, remote control, and monitoring of the home environment whilst using the internet as the communication backbone [7]. Technically the home automation system consists of five separate blocks: the devices that are under control, the devices containing sensors and actuators, the network through which all the devices are being controlled, the controller, and the remote-controlled devices [8]. In Fig. (**2**) shown below, the IoT devices can be any smart home appliances ranging from electric kettles to smart TV's, from humidity sensors to smart home security monitoring cameras, from smart gardening to smart central heating of homes, from RFIDs to smart wearables, from smart door locks to personal AI assistants such as Amazon's Alexa. The IoT gateway interacts between different types of communication technologies which may vary in different protocols and establishes a bridge between the IoT devices and the internet. Prior to sending the data onwards through the internet, the gateway aggregates all the data it receives from the devices, translates the sensors protocols, and performs the pre-processing of data. The IoT devices connect to the IoT gateway using wireless transmission modes such as Bluetooth, ZigBee, LTE, or Wi-Fi, followed by bridging them further onto the public cloud [9]. Finally, all the collected data travels to the specified web servers or the customized IoT applications which perform the analysis on the collected real-time monitoring data as well as perform the required actions. An example of said actions is lowering and adjusting the temperature and humidity of the home environment after being detected as high by the sensors, and further enhancing the onboard intelligence to change the temperature to the same settings every day at this very specific time, Fig (**2**).

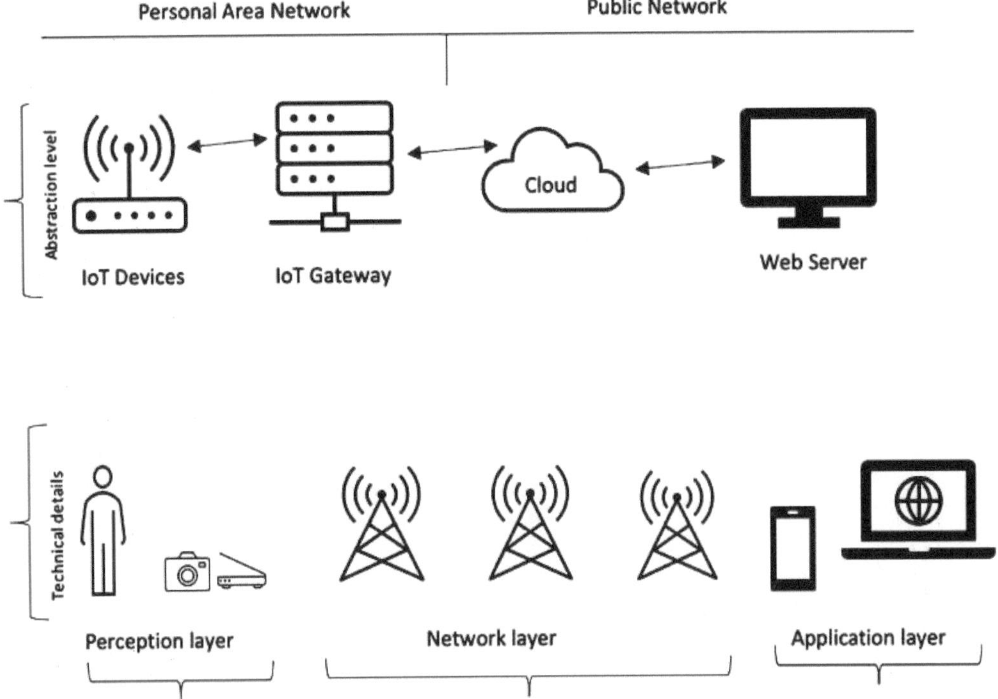

Fig. (2). A typical Smart home architecture portraying how the communication takes place between each component of the architecture [10].

3. SECURITY VULNERABILITIES, THREATS AND RISKS

As IoT has evolved in bringing about hundreds of new IoT devices that have not actually been tested or verified by any regulatory authority, so have the number of security threats increasing exponentially, providing a greater attack surface for the cyber-criminals. Several other factors have contributed to the exponential growth: the insecure configuration of IoT devices that can be directly accessible from the internet, and the lack of security updates that in turn leave devices vulnerable to zero-day attacks [11]. The Internet of Things and Security are often not found in the same place. Many problems have been seen with personal data being leaked, invasion of privacy, and the data being encrypted and locked up. This is mostly because manufacturers don't pay special attention to the security of these IoT devices.

3.1. Vulnerabilities & Threats

Vulnerabilities are loopholes in a system or design that allow a user to gain unauthorized access or conduct malicious activities. Vulnerabilities exist in many areas of the IoT environments, existing mostly in the hardware or software, in the policies or procedures used in the systems, or the weaknesses of the users themselves. System hardware and software are the two main components that every IoT system is based on Table **1**. The vulnerabilities detected in hardware are difficult to identify and resolve whereas the software vulnerabilities can mostly be found in operating systems, software applications, and other control software. There are several factors that lead to the design flaws in the software: human error, the complexity of the software itself, poor and ineffective communication between the developers and the users, or the lack of skills and knowledge [12].

Table 1. The vulnerabilities that could possibly be found in smart homes, their corresponding security attacks, and the countermeasures against them [5].

Attack Type	Device Vulnerabilities	Potential Countermeasures
Device software failure	Integer/buffer overflows	Static/dynamic verification techniques
Node tampering attack	Manual hardware tampering/replacement	Tamper proofing techniques (*e.g.*, usage of PUFs)
Eaves dropping attack	Unencrypted communication channel	Lightweight cryptographic encryption techniques
Malicious code injection	Lack of software integrity checks, insecure software APIs	Chain of trust, API endpoint security (*e.g.*, input validation)
Unauthorized access	Hardware/Software vulnerabilities	Timely OTA updates, secure session key generation
Social engineering attack	Weak password protection	Strong password protection, two-factor authentication
Device hardware exploitation	Open, insecure hardware interfaces (*e.g.*, JTAG, USB ports)	Secure-by-design (*e.g.*, access restrictions, adhering to industry standards)
Malicious node insertion	Weak encryption schemes	Device identity management system, symmetric key encryption

3.2. Weak Credentials

The most common and prevailing vulnerability was found to be weak authentication conFigd for devices. Most of the devices were running with the default usernames and passwords [13], whereas the rest were either easily guessable, hardcoded, or passwords in unencrypted form. By using strong password guidelines, the device can be better protected against brute-force attacks [5]. Shodan is a famous search engine for scanning IoT devices on the internet. It conducts testing of various devices using known vulnerabilities such as default passwords along with collecting other device metadata [14]. A Mirai variant named Mukashi was found to benefit from the CVE-2020-9054 and conducted brute force attacks using default usernames and passwords to login to Zyxel NAS

Products which are Personal cloud network storage [15]. Thus the best countermeasures are to use a strong password, or better use two-factor authentication procedures and policies.

3.3. Insecure Network Services/Hardware Exploitation

Insecure network services are listed as the second most common IoT vulnerability in the article from [16]. All IoT devices need to communicate with each other over a secure communications channel. When attackers want to compromise an endpoint, the simplest way is to find vulnerabilities in the network communication running on the device. Open ports and unnecessary running services provide opportunities for attackers to gain access to the device along with providing numerous vulnerabilities to be exploited. Scanning engines such as Shodan allow to easily view open ports of nodes as well as other metadata about the device such as its type, firmware, vendor, model, or IP addresses [17, 18]. Researchers from [19] conducted an experiment on scanning open ports on an IoT device and then compromisingly it completely. Criminals may also conduct attacks by physically tampering with the device. Said attacks can be conducted by exploiting the hardware interfaces that are left unprotected by the manufacturers. Plugging in an infected USB into an open USB port on a smart thermostat, then downloading a malicious payload into the device itself, is easily accomplished. Thus, before shipping such devices manufacturers should ensure that the necessary access restrictions are put in place along with the hardware ports that should be properly secured according to the current industry standard [5].

3.4. Internal Device Failures/Limitations

The smart home device firmware or software can be potentially exploited using any of the inherent vulnerabilities to carry out a string of attacks [5]. Since a smart home compromises multiple devices, the failure of any one of those devices affects the communication and leads to the system being compromised. The failure of a smart home security camera, for instance, can cause a physical threat to the homeowner, persisting unless the device is fixed or replaced. Similarly, the malfunction of the internet or the electric power can be devastating for the entire smart-home environment as it could result in multiple device failures, the absence of real-time monitoring data, and the inability of the homeowner to have access to their home control system [20]. Since most smart home IoT devices have limited processing and memory capabilities, the majority of them are susceptible to denial of service attacks [21]. A Denial of service attack is executed on endpoints or network devices to make them unavailable for legitimate users. In an IoT environment, the hackers conducted random UDP attacks by dispatching numerous UDP packets of various sizes all at once. This resulted in the denial of services to the resources and the system [22]. In another scenario a cyber-attacker caused the target device to retransmit repeatedly, disrupting their regular transmission and causing the smart device to drain out its battery because one bit transmitted in a WSN consumes the power of the execution of 800-1000 instructions. Consequently, it led to a serious denial of services for the smart device [23]. In 2016 the well-known Mirai botnet attack was executed using approximately 65,000 IoT devices, launching in a distributed denial-of-service attack against the DNS provider Dyn [5, 13, 24]. In another vulnerability exploitation [25], demonstrated denial of service attacks using three different techniques customized for IEEE 802.15.4, also known as the foundation for ZigBee [17]. Additionally, due to the absence of data transmission protection on the main network that is used by several IoT devices in a smart home, these systems are susceptible to network layer attacks such as DoS. One of the crucial steps in fighting against such denial of service attacks is device authentication. It would protect data exchanged between the IoT devices from unauthorized access, which, as of now, has been proving to be a challenge for researchers due to the low memory and computation limits of the majority of IoT devices [20].

3.5. Insecure Ecosystem Interfaces

Securing the device itself is as essential as securing the various services and components running in the ecosystem. This could include the backend API, web application, or mobile interface in the smart home ecosystem, that may allow the compromise of the IoT device or any of its components. These could in turn introduce us to security vulnerabilities such as weak authentication controls, weak encryption in use, or unoptimised input and output filtering [16]. This can be resolved by using strong access control, along with two-factor authentication and strong encryption algorithms.

3.6. Inefficient Update Mechanisms and Insecure Components

Lack of software and firmware updates is one of the major vulnerabilities that could result in loss of data and confidentiality. Known vulnerabilities like Heartbleed [26] and Shellshock should be scanned for and patching of the device should be done accordingly. Secondly, the ability to remotely update the device should only be performed by authorized and reliable methods, such as by the manufacturer itself [16].

3.7. Risks

The general security risks found in a typical smart home environment are listed in terms of which smart devices they could occur from and the countermeasures to be safe from such risks.

4. BUSINESS CONTINUITY AND DISASTER RECOVERY

Business continuity refers to devising a plan of action in case your organization suffers a disruption that is caused by some kind of natural disaster or a cyber incident. The business continuity plan would then assist the organization in keeping the functions going, as well as dealing with cyber threats. The most common cyber threats include denial of service, a data breach, or a ransomware attack. Once said attacks occur, the normal business functions are severely disrupted. Quickly recovering from such business interruptions is essential for the survival of the business itself. A disaster recovery plan, on the other hand, highlights the corrective controls that must be taken once an incident has taken place. This is a primarily reactive approach, whereas the business continuity plan might reduce or eliminate the impact before the disaster occurs [27]. As the technologies evolve, they bring about various new vulnerabilities and threats that may affect the results of a risk assessment. As predicted by experts, the increase in damages to a corporation is due to its poor Business Continuity approaches [28]. Various reports show the influences of IoT are causing changes in how businesses operate and grow. As IoT relies heavily on a network through which data is exchanged, every organization needs to manage these networks so that they do not infringe on the privacy laws in their country of residence. For this reason, Business continuity plans need to be prepared so that the network services can be protected from internal/external threats along with their impact on the IoT business processes [29].

IoT devices can be extremely effective in assisting with disaster recovery as the huge amounts of data that is collected by these devices, combined and then analyzed by Artificial Intelligence, can create very useful statistics for future predictions about disasters. IoT devices would definitely save us a lot of time, effort and money in generating such data for us as the devices are integrated into our lives today.

5. ORGANIZATIONAL SECURITY, AWARENESS AND INFORMATION SHARING

A smart home gives extensive access to many parts of our daily lives remotely. Although intended for the convenience of the homeowner it could also be exploited by people with malicious intentions. To be best prepared and protected against the ever-growing threats of today's world in the Home automation sector, there are several recommendations that one could follow. Whichever IoT devices are added in the smart home should properly be conFigd with separate usernames and passwords, where the passwords are based on best practice guidelines, and the usernames are not easy to guess. The IoT devices must be upgraded to the latest software or firmware available to fix the existing and known vulnerabilities. Moreover, all existing devices must be patched regularly and the core network that connects all these IoT devices should be segmented for the containment of any cyber incident damage to be as less as possible. All devices should be mapped so that their current credentials, firmware versions, and patches are known to the home user and can be replaced or upgraded anytime. The main router should be properly customized and not just be running using the default setting, as that is usually the primary and most important device uniting all IoT devices with each other. Two-Factor authentication must be enabled on supported devices. Open ports and the running of unnecessary services should be regularly scanned and closed off to lessen the surface attack to the minimum. The usage of strong encryption on your Wi-Fi should be implemented and a guest network should be set up for guests to provide them with limited and temporary access to your internal network. An Uninterruptible Power Supply might come in handy to avoid any loss of power, as power outages might disrupt the security of your smart home thereby affecting the physical security of your home. As a best practice, a VPN should be used so that all your network traffic whether internal or external is encrypted protecting your communications from Man in the Middle attacks and Eavesdropping attacks. Branded IoT devices should be considered instead of buying cheap and unknown devices as the larger manufacturers invest more in the security of the IoT device rather than just the sales. An In-hub security manager for your IoT network could greatly assist and automate the urgently required tasks such as patching vulnerabilities and managing the passwords for the individual devices. All manufacturers should follow a standardized procedure for quality assurance dedicating sufficient time and resources for it.

CONCLUSION

Generally smart home automation devices lack security, as the intense competition in the increase of sales of IoT devices has forced manufacturers to focus more on quantity and variety rather than on quality. The common vulnerabilities, risks, and attacks discussed can be effectively mitigated by constantly patching and scanning your IoT devices as well as by other mentioned methods. Using best practice techniques in protecting your core network and all your devices conFigd in your home is the way to a secure and stable smart home. This study aimed to discuss the most common security threats and their effective countermeasures.

REFERENCES

[1] A.D. Rayome, *How the term 'Internet of Things' was invented,* 2018.https://www.techrepublic.com/article/how-the-term-internet-of-things-was-invented

[2] "The IoT Data Explosion: How Big Is the IoT Data Market?, " [Online]. Available:

https://priceonomics.com/the-iot-data-explosion-how-big-is-the-iot-data [Accessed: 29 October 2020]. [Online].

[3] A. Roy, "Why IoT Smart Home Automation is in Demand", redappletech.com, 12 April 2019. [Online]. Available: https://www.redappletech.com/why-iot-smart-home-automation-is-in-demand/ [Accessed: 30 October 2020].

[4] "80 Wicked & Insightful IoT Statistics" 25 february 25, 2021. [Online]. Available: https://safeatlast.co/blog/iot-statistics [Accessed: 31 October 2020].

[5] T. Alladi, V. Chamola, B. Sikdar, and K.K.R. Choo, "Consumer IoT: Security vulnerability case studies and solutions", *IEEE Consum. Electron. Mag.,* vol. 9, no. 2, pp. 17-25, 2020. [http://dx.doi.org/10.1109/MCE.2019.2953740]

[6] L. Costa, J. P. Barros, and M. Tavares, "Vulnerabilities in IoT devices for smart home environment", *In: ICISSP 2019 - Proceedings of the 5th International Conference on Information Systems Security and Privacy,* pp. 615-622, 2019.

[7] V. Fabi, G. Spigliantini, and S.P. Corgnati, "Insights on Smart Home Concept and Occupants' Interaction with Building Controls", *Energy. Procedia,* vol. 111, pp. 759-769, 2017. [http://dx.doi.org/10.1016/j.egypro.2017.03.238]

[8] O. Kyas, O. "How To Smart Home - A Step by Step Guide Using Internet, Z-Wave, KNX & OpenRemote". *Key Concept.* 1st. Key Concept Press: Wyk, Germany, 2014, pp. 23-27.

[9] "What is an IoT Gateway?, " 25th September 2019 [Online]. Available: https://www.lanner-america.com/blog/what-is-an-iot-gateway [Accessed: 31 October 2020].

[10] B. Ali, and A. I. Awad, "Cyber and physical security vulnerability assessment for IoT-based smart homes", *Open Access,* vol. 18, no. 3, pp. 1-17, 2018. [http://dx.doi.org/10.3390/s18030817]

[11] A. Pinto, "What IT Needs to Know about OT/IoT Security Threats in 2020", Jul 21, 2020. [Online]. Available https: // www.nozominetworks.com/blog/ what- it- needs-to-know-about-ot-io-se-urity-threats-in-2020 [Accessed: 31 October 2020].

[12] J.M. Kizza, *Guide to Computer Network Security.* 5th ed. Springer International Publishing: Cham, 2020, pp. 60-100. [http://dx.doi.org/10.1007/978-3-030-38141-7]

[13] "2020 Unit 42 IoT Threat Report" 10 March 2020, Palo Alto. [Online]. Available: https://drive.google.com/open?id=1VLA1IweXyJMVeWxvy_8vwtypUQXB_Uhn [Accessed: 28 October 2020].

[14] "Search Engine for the Internet of Everything" Shodan (2013). [Online]. https://www.shodan.io [Accessed: 1 November 2020].

[15] "Smart Yet Flawed: IoT Device Vulnerabilities Explained - Security News", May 28 2020. [Online]. Available: https://www.trendmicro.com/vinfo/us/security/news/internet-of-things/smart-yet-fl-wed-iot-device-vulnerabilities-explained [Accessed: 1 November 2020].

[16] "OWASP Internet of Things," 2018. [Online]. Available: https://owasp.org/www-project-internet-of-things/ [Accessed: 1 November 2020].

[17] R. Heartfield, G. Loukas, S. Budimir, A. Bezemskij, J.R.J. Fontaine, A. Filippoupolitis, and E. Roesch, "A taxonomy of cyber-physical threats and impact in the smart home", *Comput. Secur.* , vol. 78, no. Sep, pp. 398-428, 2018.https://www.sciencedirect.com/science/article/pii/S0167404818304875 [http://dx.doi.org/10.1016/j.cose.2018.07.011]

[18] H. Lin and N W. Bergmann, "IoT privacy and security challenges for smart home environments", Information. vol. 7, no. 3, pp. 44 , 2016. [Online]. Available from: https://www.mdpi.com/2078-2489/7/3/44 [Accessed: 28 October 2020].

[19] I. Astaburuaga, A. Lombardi, B.L. Torre, and S. Hughes, "Vulnerability analysis of ar.drone 2.0, an

embedded linux system:", *2019 IEEE 9th Annual Computing and Communication Workshop and Conference (CCWC),*, Las Vegas, NV, USA, pp. 7-9, 2019.

[20] K. Karimi, K. and S. Krit, “Smart home-smartphone systems: Threats, security requirements and open research challenges”: *2019International Conference of Computer Science and Renewable Energies (ICCSRE)*, 22-24 July 2019, Agadir, Morocco.

[21] M. Abomhara, and G.M. Køien, "Cyber security and the internet of things: Vulnerabilities, threats, intruders and attacks", *J. Cyber Secur. Mobil.,* vol. 4, no. 1, pp. 65-88, 2014. [http://dx.doi.org/10.13052/jcsm2245-1439.414]

[22] A. Bijalwan, M. Wazid, E.S. Pilli, and R.C. Joshi, *Forensics of Random-UDP Flooding Attacks,* 2015.https://www.proquest.com/docview/1686228040 [http://dx.doi.org/10.4304/jnw.10.5.287-293]

[23] H.S. Kim, M.P. Andersen, K. Chen, S. Kumar, W.J. Zhao, K. Ma, and D.E. Culler, "System Architecture Directions for Post-SoC/32-bit Networked Sensors", *SenSys '18: Proceedings of the 16th ACM Conference on Embedded Networked Sensor Systems,* 2018 Shenzhen, China. [http://dx.doi.org/10.1145/3274783.3274839]

[24] M. Yu, J. Zhuge, M. Cao, Z. Shi, and L. Jiang, "A Survey of Security Vulnerability Analysis, Discovery, Detection, and Mitigation on IoT Devices", *Fut. Int.,* vol. 12, no. 2, 2020. https://www.mdpi.com/1999-5903/12/2/27 [http://dx.doi.org/10.3390/fi12020027]

[25] P. Jokar, H. Nicanfar, and V.C.M. Leung, *Model-based Intrusion Detection for Home Area Networks in Smart Grids,* 2011.https://ieeexplore.ieee.org/document/6102320

[26] "OpenSSL ‘Heartbleed’ vulnerability (CVE-2014-0160)”, October 05, 2016. [Online]. Available. us-cert.cisa.gov/ncas/alerts/TA14-098A [Accessed: 1 November 2020].

[27] V. Cerullo, and M.J. Cerullo, "Business Continuity Planning: A Comprehensive Approach", *Inform. System. Management,* vol. 21, no. 3, pp. 70-78, 2006. www.tandfonline.com

[28] S.A. Torabi, H.R. Soufi, and N. Sahebjamnia, "A New Framework for Business Impact Analysis in Business Continuity Management (with a Case Study)", *Safety. Sci.,* vol. 68, pp. 309-323, 2014. [http://dx.doi.org/10.1016/j.ssci.2014.04.017]

[29] J.A. Ali, Q. Nasir, and F.T. Dweiri, "Business continuity framework for Internet of Things (IoT) Services", *Int. J. Syst. Assur. Eng. Manag.,* vol. 11, no. 6, pp. 1380-1394, 2020. [http://dx.doi.org/10.1007/s13198-020-01005-7]

CHAPTER 5

IoT Policy and Governance Reference Architecture: Integrity and Security of Information Across IoT Devices

Yap Chi Yew[1], **Intan Farahana Kamsin**[1] and **Nur Khairunnisha Zainal**[1,*]

[1] *School of Computing & Technology, Asia Pacific University of Technology and Innovation, Kuala Lumpur, Malaysia*

Abstract: The Internet of Things (IoT) technology has been applied to our daily life infrastructure to make our lives easier and more comfortable. However, various variations in the IoT reference architecture represent that the developers need to be aware in order to implement the technology in a secure and accurate form. The knowledge of these reference architectures is important as they provide the guidelines for IoT developers and enterprises to develop high-quality IoT products. Requirements such as security, data process, and privacy issues must always be concerned. The reference architectures are used in the development of IoT products. This paper discusses and explores IoT-related field topics ranging from IoT reference architecture to policy to governance. Different kinds of variations in the reference architecture and the IoT governance policy are discussed to ensure the integrity and security of information transmitted across devices in the IoT ecosystem.

Keywords: Architecture, Governance, IoT, Policy.

1. INTRODUCTION

The implementation of IoT technology is growing immensely nowadays. The overwhelming use of technology by humanity should be considered from fair management architectures under major governance. Therefore, IoT management and governance are paramount to be enforced on those who is directly or indirectly benefited from the technology currently and in the future. The architecture was designed to ensure that connectivity, data processing, and security systems of IoT technology can provide a reference architecture to solve the complexities and management of the IoT. Governance is vital to control the

* **Corresponding author Nur Khairunnisha Zainal:** School of Computing & Technology, Asia Pacific University of Technology and Innovation, Kuala Lumpur, Malaysia; E-mail: khairunnisha.zainal@staffemail.apu.edu.my

Muhammad Ehsan Rana & Manoj Jayabalan (Eds.)

IoT technology development today [1 - 5]. IoT policy is needed to monitor the development of IoT technology. Therefore, we need to study how management and governance work and affect the IoT technology.

2. REFERENCE ARCHITECTURE OF IOT

Reference architecture is usually a model framework architecture that is suitable and adaptive to be repeated over time. IoT technology needs architecture to be managed because the old IT technology is based on fragmented software implementations which proved to be difficult for monitoring and controlling in the past [1]. An architecture is introduced to serve as a guidance standard to make the management work easier than before. There are big requirements for reference architecture of IoT technology in the enterprise to make the development more tangible and profitable [1]. Therefore, some variations and innovations have evolved the reference architecture currently, to fit the ecosystem of IoT that keeps changing according to times. The evolved reference architectures that are commonly used today are Internet of Things-Architecture (IoT-A), Industrial Internet Reference Architecture (IIRA), and Service-Oriented Architecture (SOA). These reference architectures are purposed to assist interoperability, monitor invention, and moderate usage of IoT technology, Fig. (**1**).

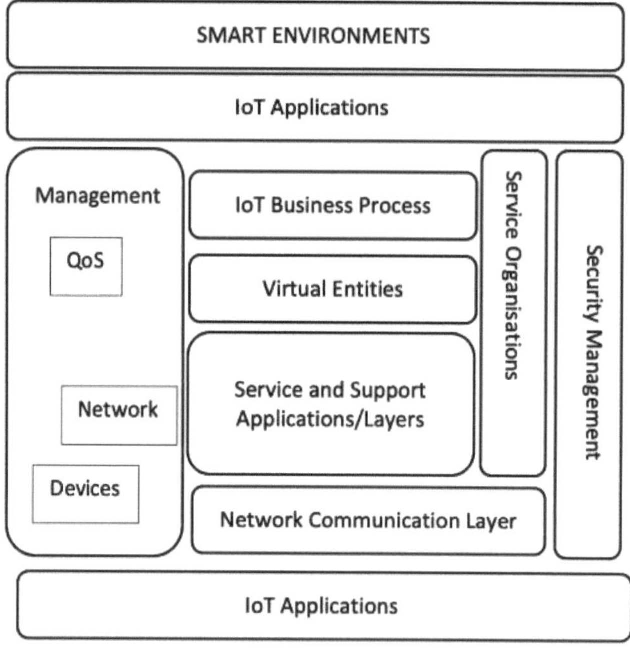

Fig. (1). Internet of things—architecture (IoT-A) [2].

Internet of Things—Architecture (IoT-A) gives a comprehensive view of the data and information of IoT technology [1]. IoT-A is greatly used in today's development environments due to its advantages. The IoT-A focuses on the common aspects of informatics instead of the usage of the IoT technology [2]. This situation can let developers who use IoT-A design to develop specific IoT devices for a wider range of usages. Hence, these kinds of IoT devices are designed to be suitable for the transformation of data as well as information usage, which is a major part of IoT technology nowadays. Furthermore, the IoT-A widely encompasses abstract modelling and structuring of IoT business process management, resources, and services from the angles of information and functionality [1]. For instance, cloud servers are implemented for server management but the IoT devices of users are used in domain-specific computers. IoT-A has management mechanisms and security protocols implemented across IoT devices [1]. For example, Hypertext Transfer Protocol Secure (HTTPS) is used to safeguard the data transmission of IoT devices. EXI (Efficient XML Interchange) is implemented for managing the exchange of data on IoT devices. These mechanisms and protocols that are used in IoT-A have greatly benefited the development of IoT technology. Therefore, these excellent features have made the IoT-A a good managing architecture for the development of IoT technology.

Industrial Internet Reference Architecture (IIRA) mainly focuses on the usability of IoT technology for the industry sector and the interoperability among industries [3]. Thus, IIRA can focus more on industry and business use cases. IIRA also has management mechanisms and security protocols like IoT-A implemented across IoT devices. Four important viewpoints that build up the IIRA: Business Viewpoint, Usage Viewpoint, Functional Viewpoint, and Implementation Viewpoint [3]. The Business Viewpoint is defined as the clients and their business perspectives, targets, and benefits [3]. The Usage Viewpoint is the expectation of the IoT technology in the industry to provide the expected market goals and targets. Furthermore, Implementation Viewpoint describes the necessity of implementation of the respective IoT technology for the respective functional usages. Said uses include the communication system, data rates of the system, and other technical features. Lastly, Functional Viewpoint is known for the functional elements along with the connection and interaction among the IoT devices in the ecosystem [3]. This Functional Viewpoint lets the IoT devices connect among themselves to complete the operations and tasks that can help humans. These four essential viewpoints make IIRA greatly used in the industry sector to manage and control IoT technology more efficiently.

Service Oriented Architecture (SOA) combines IoT technology into service-based connectivity that is agile and reusable, focusing on the end-users, Fig. (**2**) [4]. SOA is an architecture that combines large scale private and public IoT systems and other tools of computing with a continual progression of phenomenal advent recently. SOA not only relates to the communication part of technology but also lines up the business processes to improve the decision making and working efficiency of the end-users. SOA can be varied according to different environments, but its basic idea contains three basic components: the registry, the provider, and the requester [4]. The registry is known as the service broker which makes the service description and access information available. The provider is responsible to register the respective service at the registry and provide the respective service to the end-users. The requester is the end-user that seeks the services with the aid of the registry. The SOA is very simple to be implemented by companies and enterprises to provide and manage IoT services for their clients. Therefore, many companies and enterprises such as IBM, Microsoft and others use SOA to provide cloud services for IoT users, because SOA can help developers to send, store, and share data and information for developing IoT devices together [4]. Hence, SOA has become a great reference architecture for IoT technology recently.

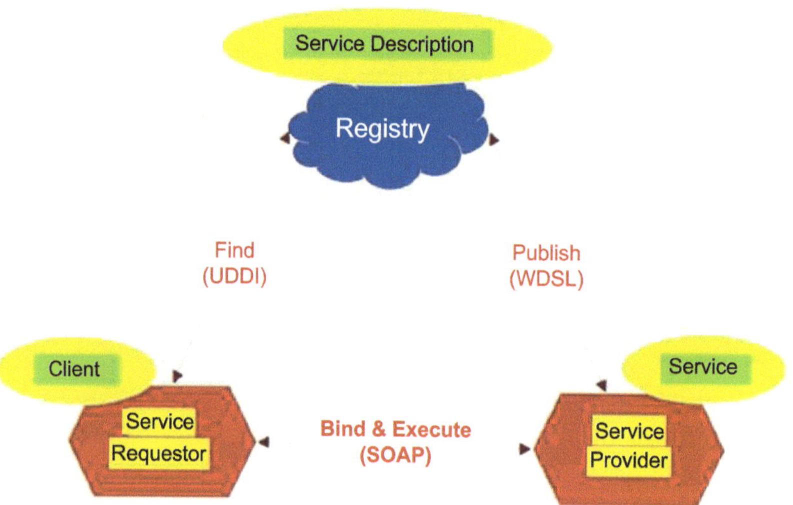

Fig. (2). Service Oriented Architecture (SOA) [4].

3. IOT POLICY

The IoT Technology is the digital ecosystem that changes rapidly in this era. Policies are needed to govern the development of IoT technology, to make sure its evolution can contribute to mankind. The rationale for IoT policy is to have proper governance of the IoT devices, especially in a well-developed nation [5]. There are some main objectives to set up the policies for the IoT. The first objective of the IoT policy is to make sure that the IoT technology is profitable for all layers of users [5]. The next objective is to enhance the lives of humans by using IoT technology. For instance, a resident can live more comfortably and conveniently in a smart home rather than a conventional home. The third objective is that the research and development of IoT technology should be efficient and environmentally friendly all the time [5]. The rationale for this situation is to prevent any IoT devices to lead to environmental pollution and damage to our current living environments. The final objective of IoT policy is to make sure the IoT technology is always safe to use by the people. Data and information of the users should always be safeguarded by security systems to prevent users from suffering from physical and mental damages. These are the objectives for the people to set the IoT policy to govern the IoT technology.

4. IOT GOVERNANCE

There are some different types of governance which are known as data governance, IT governance and IoT governance. Data governance is focusing on data asset management and monitoring, which includes the life cycle of data from the data acquisition to deletion of data [6]. Thus, data governance needs to establish the standards and protocols for the data management procedures such as data transmission, data storing, data backup, *etc.* Effective data governance can allow a company or enterprise to make accurate predictions and decisions after the data has transformed into useful information and knowledge.

IT governance is defined as governing of the IT resources [6]. Examples of IT resources are network communication, hardware requirement, software requirement, databases and more. These resources need to have complete governance to work together properly and efficiently, as the company or enterprise will suffer from a great loss if the IT resources are broken or damaged due to not governing properly. Therefore, some IT governance frameworks are introduced: Control Objectives for Information and Related Technology (COBIT), Information Technology Infrastructure Library (ITIL) and ISO 27001. Said frameworks are there to let people know how to have the right methods of IT governance [6].

IoT governance is an extension of IT governance. It addresses the lifecycles of IoT devices and the integration of data governance, as IoT devices must manage large amounts of data [6]. IoT governance ensures that IT governance and data governance work together to support the development of the IoT technology ecosystem. This is because IoT devices require data to function. IoT devices are constantly transmitting data to communicate with each other. IoT devices collect data from users and upload it to cloud servers, where it is analyzed using IoT technology. Therefore, IoT governance is used to govern IoT technology to make it more user-friendly and to help users transition more easily from traditional methods.

5. FRAMEWORK (IDENTIFY, INSULATE, INSPECT AND IMPROVE FRAMEWORK)

The 4I Framework is used to govern IoT technology. It is known as Identify, Insulate, Inspect, and Improve Framework [6]. IoT technology ecosystem used this 4I Framework to have a more convenient way to govern the data asset [6]. The first "I" in the 4I Framework is the Identify Phase. It can determine the true service provider to protect the data and information of users from being endangered by others. The second "I" is the Insulate Phase. This phase lets the protective operations take place to reduce the risks of user data being leaked or hacked. Actions that are taken in this phase are data encryption, frequent update of the security system of cloud servers, and more. The third "I" is the Inspect Phase. It focuses on the integration of sophisticated real-time tracking, auditing, and reporting [6]. Any personally identifiable information (PII) data that is unencrypted must be encrypted before storing in databases. Moreover, a robust asset management software is implemented to record the data stored in databases [6]. The fourth "I" is the Improve Phase. This phase allows the companies and enterprises to set up suitable policies and standards to enhance the governance of the IoT technology. Improvements in IoT technology are made to help us gain better benefits for our future. Therefore, governance of IoT technology is paramount to make sure the IoT technology is always feeding our human civilization with advantages.

CONCLUSION

Management and governance play vital purposes in the IoT ecosystem of enterprises, as laws and policies are established to control and monitor their development. Safety and security issues can be strengthened and guarded with standards and rules for IoT technology. Variations in the reference architecture are important as the guidelines for the IoT developers and enterprises are to develop high-quality products. Requirements such as security, data process, and privacy issues must always be concerned, along with following the reference architectures in the development of IoT products. Governance is essential to guide the growth of the ecosystem of enterprise IoT. People need to know the changes in data governance, IT governance and IoT governance. The 4I framework is very useful in the governance of IoT development nowadays because this framework is used to enhance the efforts of governance of IoT technology from many aspects . Therefore, management and governance are paramount in the ecosystem of enterprise IoT.

REFERENCES

[1] M. Weyrich, and C. Ebert, "Reference Architectures for the Internet of Things", *IEEE Softw.,* vol. 33, no. 1, pp. 112-116, 2016.
[http://dx.doi.org/10.1109/MS.2016.20]

[2] P. P. Ray, "A Survey on Internet of Things Architectures", *2018 IEEE 9th Annual Information Technology, Electronics and Mobile Communication Conference (IEMCON),* vol. 30, Vancouver, BC, Canada, no. 3, pp. 291-391, 2018.
[http://dx.doi.org/10.1109/IEMCON.2018.8614931]

[3] D. G. S. Pivoto, L. F. F. de Almeida, R. da Rosa Righi, J. J. P. C. Rodrigues, A. B. Lugli, and A. M. Alberti, "Cyber-physical Systems Architectures for Industrial Internet of Things Applications in Industry 4.0: A Literature Review", *J. Manuf. Sys.,* vol. 58, pp. 176-192, 2021.
[http://dx.doi.org/10.1016/j.jmsy.2020.11.017]

[4] A. Bamhdi, "Requirements capture and comparative analysis of open source *versus* proprietary service oriented architecture", *Comput. Stand. Interfaces,* vol. 74, p. 103468., 2021.
[http://dx.doi.org/10.1016/j.csi.2020.103468]

[5] S. Chatterjee, and A.K. Kar, "Regulation and governance of the Internet of Things in India", *Digital Policy, Regulation and Governance,* vol. 20, no. 5, pp. 399-412, 2018.
[http://dx.doi.org/10.1108/DPRG-04-2018-0017]

[6] A. Dasgupta, A. Gill, and F. Hussain, "A Conceptual Framework for Data Governance in IoT-enabled Digital IS Ecosystems", *Proceedings of the 8th International Conference on Data Science, Technology and Applications,* pp. 209-216, 2019.
[http://dx.doi.org/10.5220/0007924302090216]

CHAPTER 6

Organizational Security Improvement in Preventing Deepfake Ransomware

Janesh Kapoor[1] and **Nor Azlina Abdul Rahman**[2,*]

[1] *School of Computing & Technology, Asia Pacific University of Technology and Innovation, Kuala Lumpur, Malaysia*

[2] *Forensic and Cyber Security Research Centre, Asia Pacific University of Technology and Innovation, Kuala Lumpur, Malaysia*

Abstract: Ransomware is one of the most popular threats in the cyber world. There is an emerging technique for integrating artificial intelligence (AI), deep machine learning, and facial mapping for creating fake videos of people doing and saying something that they have not actually done. Deepfake ransomware is an attack where deepfake technology is being used in ransomware campaigns. Anyone can become the victim or target of this attack, however, this research paper focuses on the impact of deepfake ransomware on organisations. It covers potential risks that an organization might face due to deepfake ransomware attacks such as customer trust, organization reputation, and many other impacts. Besides that, this paper also discusses defence techniques that an organization could consider implementing in protecting the organization against deepfake ransomware attacks. Implementing the defence without awareness will not be effective, hence it is highlighted several times in this paper, that awareness is needed amongst the employees and employers to prevent the organisation from deepfake ransomware. Additionally, it also mentions possible risk management, business continuity, and disaster recovery plans that should be considered by the organization whilst handling the situation of deepfake ransomware attacks.

Keywords: Deepfake ransomware, Organizational security, Security awareness, Risk management, Business continuity.

1. INTRODUCTION

With the use of machine learning technology and artificial intelligence integration, deepfakes have been increasingly difficult to capture as an attack, because deepfake videos are seemingly authentic. Attackers use such attacks as ransomware towards organisations [1 - 3]. For instance, an attacker creates deepfake videos of an organization in which the CEO talks about the company

* **Corresponding author Nor Azlina Abdul Rahman:** Forensic and Cyber Security Research Centre, Asia Pacific University of Technology and Innovation, Kuala Lumpur, Malaysia; E-mail: nor.azlina@apu.edu.my

Muhammad Ehsan Rana & Manoj Jayabalan (Eds.)

and announces insolvency. The attacker then uses the material to threaten the organization until the ransom is paid. If the ransom is not paid, the attacker may release the material to the media or publish it on social media channels. This research discusses the impact and potential risks to the organization, business continuity, risk management, and disaster recovery measures taken by the organization. Additionally, it covers defense techniques for improving organizational security to prevent deepfake ransomware, as well as information sharing and awareness of deepfake ransomware.

1.1. What is Deepfake?

Deepfakes are defined as computer-generated images, videos, and voices that are made to imitate the biometric characteristics of a person. Characteristic details such as facial expressions, appearances, and voices are manipulated with detail that makes deepfakes believable [4]. The phrase deepfake is a combination of the terms ‘deep learning’ and ‘fake’. Deep learning refers to the arrangement of algorithms that allow the software to learn and make intelligent decisions on its own [5 - 7].

1.2. How Deepfakes are Created?

Deepfakes rely on machine learning, which uses two networks that are fed the same data sets and compared against each other. Deepfakes are created using a machine learning tool called generative adversarial networks (GANs) [8, 9]. Generative adversarial networks consist of two machine learning models, one of which trains itself to create and imitate using massive data sets, whilst the other detects the imitation that was created. This is done until the first model creates an imitation that is unrecognizable to each other [10, 11]. Hence, deepfake videos are manipulated with the use of Artificial Intelligence (AI) and Machine Learning (ML). Contrary to this, ransomware is a form of malware that prevents victims from accessing their personal data unless the ransom is paid [11].

Ransomware refers to a deepfake video with voice mimicking capabilities that appear to be genuine. However, the deepfakes that are made could be of malicious intent and include pornographic videos or a CEO's speech about insolvency to an organisation. Therefore, deepfake tech can be used in ransomware campaigns or *vice versa*.

1.3. Why Deepfakes were Created?

Deepfakes used to be of good intent such as mimicking someone in a funny perspective. The technology of deepfakes is still being used in the film industry for 3d movies, animations and special effects [12]. However, cybercriminals have turned this technology into malicious ware. As deepfake uses fake content to deceive its viewers, it is used to spread misinformation and other malicious data. In the past, only people with specialised skills were able to create such content. Unfortunately, the ever-rising race in technology and the ease of obtaining such technology have made it easy for anyone to use [13]. The instigation of machine learning and smartphone apps such as ReFace, Face Swap Live, Snapchat, and others has allowed anyone with a smartphone to create deepfakes.

This poses a major threat to any business or organisation, as it can incite panic and misinformation to produce harmful outcomes [14 - 16]. Thus, the deepfake's malicious intentions to organisations are to spread scams or hoaxes, incite pornography, for social engineering manipulation, and to identity theft, and financial fraud. An example of said financial fraud is how voice skins are used to create audio deepfakes that pose as legitimate, and, in turn, prove to be a threat to CEOs of organisations. An example is the case of a chief executive of the firm's German parent company, which demanded a fraudulent transfer of $243,000 [17].

2. DEEPFAKE RANSOMWARE IMPACT AND POTENTIAL RISK TO THE ORGANIZATION

Deepfake ransomware generates negative impacts and potential risks to an organisation. As compared to the traditional threat of fake news, deepfakes are harder to detect, thus, leading people to dismiss genuine footage as fake. As an attacker creates deepfakes of an organisation, competitors may use this to their advantage as consumers lose the trust of the organisation. Furthermore, brand sabotage, blackmails, financial fraud, and others would be incriminating to an organization [18]. Due to the current pandemic of COVID-19, workplaces are conducted virtually. With this digital transition, the increase of video conferencing and other digital tools gives more access to deepfake material to be created more deceivably [19].

The CIA triad, confidentiality, integrity, and availability, of information security, is an organisation's pride to protect. This shows the organisation manages its CIA to gain the trust and loyalty of its customers and stakeholders. Thus, the deepfake ransomware attack scatters the CIA of an organisation's responsibility to its customers and stakeholders, resulting in impacting the organisation [20 - 22]. The impact on an organisation and the potential risk may include:

2.1. Customer's Trust and Confidence

A customer's trust and confidence is an organisation's main priority, and any deepfake ransomware or disinformation would result in the loss of it. Moreover, the irrefutable damage would have the organisation in disarray to gain its integrity for its customers. Thus, the loss of business and customer acquisition would be high [23].

2.2. Social Engineering

With the usual means of attacks such as spam, phishing, malware, and man-i--the-middle, deepfake ransomware provides an unprecedented means of mimicking individuals [8]. With the contribution of fraud that targets specific individuals, the attackers use deepfake voices or videos to influence employees with legitimacy [1]. Therefore, this could lead to leaking of sensitive data, possible financial theft, or disinformation.

2.3. C-Level Fraud

An attacker can use deepfake technology to pose as C-level management to persuade employees of an organisation into believing it is legit. Once successful, the attacker can demand anything from its employees. Furthermore, with deepfake videos posing as C-level management, operational matters are affected by disinformation and fake statements such as insolvency to cause discrimination towards an organisation [24].

2.4. Extortion Against Influential Business Leaders

Deepfake videos that were created against influential business leaders in the organisation can be used by attackers to extort them in return for a reward such as ransomware. As they are influential business leaders, the attackers gain leverage over them, making it easier for the attackers to extort them [12].

2.5. Tarnish Organisation's Reputation

Deepfake ransomware videos of an organisation's C-level management that has incriminating information, will tarnish the organization's reputation if the video delivers misinformation. This is related to identity theft as the attackers source online data of a certain individual to create a deepfake video. With the fraudulent video looking legitimate, the message delivered could be malicious towards the organisation; demoting the brand name and products, or resulting in a data breach or insolvency of a customer [12]. Thus, the public opinion of the video would be swayed due to its influential C-level management, impacting the organisation's reputation [1].

2.6. Operational Impact

The impact of deepfake ransomware on an organization is felt both at the zero hour of the attack and at the end. Multiple uses of deepfakes can lead to zero-hour attacks, where the deepfake is believed to be legitimate and can cause shipments, orders, deliveries, productions, and other daily operations to be changed according to the attacker's wishes. The second impact is realized when it is too late, and can have a significant financial burden if the attack is not caught early [17].

2.7. Market Stock Manipulation

With the volatility of the stock market, deepfakes have the significance to manipulate the market according to the attacker. This could either raise or crash the market value. Depending on the deepfake, the misinformation produced by the video such as false financial reports or lost businesses could result in massive losses for the organisation. Thus, the recovery period of such an impact is almost non-reputable [19].

2.8. The Financial Burden

Despite the financial burden that occurred in the operation impact, market stock manipulation, extortion, and fraud, the financial expenditure expands beyond the cost of recovery, compliance and fines faced from the attack. With every attack, the cost of recovery is extremely high to gain market trust. Furthermore, the cost of compliance and fines faced by the organisation depends on the breach of privacy and security [18].

2.9. Server Message Block (SMB)

Server Message Block (SMB) is a file-sharing convention, that permits Windows frameworks associated with the same organisation or space to share records. Moreover, SMB empowers computers to share printers and serial ports with other computers inside the same organisation, such as the WanaCry ransomware attack in 2017, attackers exploited the vulnerability of the Windows SMB version 1.0. This allowed remote access control for the attacker to affect the systems [6]. The attackers used the EternalBlue exploits kit to exploit the vulnerabilities in the SMBv1. Using a worm-like virus, the ransomware was able to spread across the Windows network. This ransomware attacks targeted Windows systems by encrypting data and demanding ransom payments in the Bitcoin cryptocurrency. Thus, similar ransomware attacks are possible, as there are vulnerabilities in the Windows systems.

3. RISK MANAGEMENT, BUSINESS CONTINUITY AND DISASTER RECOVERY TAKEN BY THE ORGANISATION TO HANDLE THE SITUATION

3.1. Risk Management

After any deepfake ransomware attack has occurred, a risk management business continuity and disaster recovery plan need to be taken into action for the survival of an organisation. These plans help the organisation excel from its current situation and can mitigate actions needed to be taken. Risk management is the practice of identifying potential risks in advance, analysing and implementing precautionary steps to reduce or curb the risk. Thus, risk management plans against deepfake ransomware attacks should be pre-planned [8]. To have a risk management plan against deepfake ransomware, a few key points are required to suit the organisation's needs. Therefore, risk management at every level of an organisation includes:

- Identification of the objectives of risk management should be transmitted to every level of an organisation, along with monitoring performance indicators.
- Risks that are incurred to achieve an objective must be identified, assessed, and monitored at every level of an organisation.
- By identifying the potential risk in performing a task, the responsibility of the user is to understand the outcome of the risk if performed unsuccessfully.
- Moreover, factoring in the adequacy and effectiveness of key risk indicators, risks need to be monitored continuously.

Action plans with the accountability for the management of risks should be practised and carried out, to prepare an organisation for future situations. Furthermore, the adoption of new security protocols in an organization with safety protocol acts as a combative security measure. Thereby, establishing security protocols with multiple checksums and procedure guidelines that employees follow when receiving deepfakes can be mitigated before they occur [10]. The use of risk management software facilitates following the ISO31000 and COSO standards, allows for continuous monitoring of the organisation, real-time alerts, predictive risk analysis, scenario modelling, and deepfake detections. Essentially, reducing potential future risk [3].

Employee education is a key element in being able to identify a deepfake as early as possible. With training provided, future threats are easily and quickly spotted by employees, allowing for a fast reaction plan to be carried out by an organisation [3]. Furthermore, with the use of corporate communications, organisations can mitigate deepfake ransomware threats by minimising communication channels, consistent distribution of information, centralised monitoring and reporting functions, and monitoring detection and prevention countermeasures [16].

As sensitive data is the most sought after for an attack, documentation of sensitive information such as contract agreements, financial details, and personal information of the organisation should be always kept safe. This prevents the altering of information from misleading deepfakes [19]. Moreover, as a deepfake ransomware attack involves financial damage, maintaining adequate insurance coverage of an organisation helps reduce the financial burden from insecure shareholders, customers, and recovery costs [19]. By further validating buy/sell agreements and transactions, an organisation outlines the terms and conditions agreed upon during the purchase or sales order. Thereby, any changes that are made to any agreements or new generated agreements by an attacker, will have to be further validated through various conditions. Thus, posing difficulties for a successful attack [19].

3.2. Business Continuity

According to the official standard (ISO 22301), business continuity is defined as the capability of an organisation to have continuous delivery of products and services at an acceptable predefined level following a cybercrime incident [21]. This is to ensure that the organisation operations continue despite an incident. Business continuity to an organisation is about creating a management system that prepares itself for quality response and handling of incidents, such as the current COVID-19 incident [8].

By implementing a business continuity management system, the organisation would be able to prepare itself for any incident that occurs, such as the deepfake ransomware. The goal of business continuity management is to have the organisation's operations running smoothly and limit the amount of downtime [25 - 28]. The Business Continuity Management System (BCM) consists of 7 phases: project management, risk analysis and review, business impact analysis, business continuity strategy, business continuity plan development, testing and exercising, and program management. Fig. (**1**) illustrates the business continuity management system life cycle [21].

3.2.1. Project Management (PM)

With the implementation of an Executive Management structure, an organisation can begin its first phase of the life cycle, which is project management. Project management is the implementation of an Executive Management structure and its expectations to support the BCM planning process. The inclusion of business units and functions ensures the efficiency of the tasks, project expectations, and commitments to clear roles and responsibilities. Project management establishes the need for BCM planning by researching, developing, and defining the scope and objectives of a BCM planning framework. Moreover, it manages the BCM planning process by establishing a planning committee and team, that develops an action plan to manage deadlines, along with building and maintaining teamwork using a given budget [21].

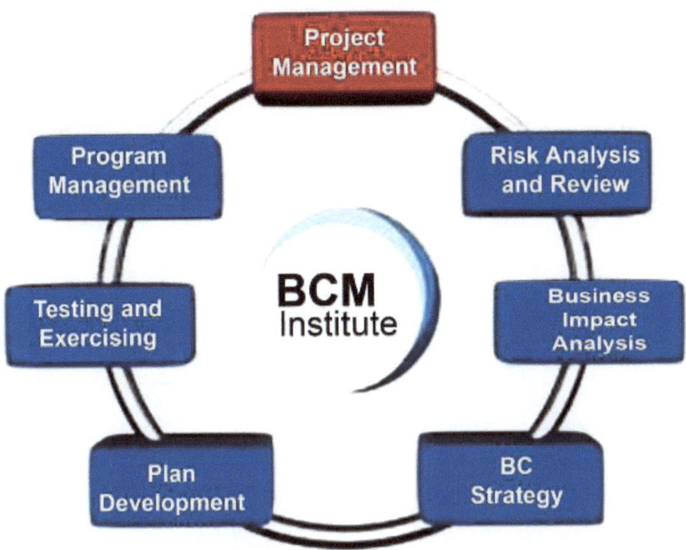

Fig. (1). Business continuity management system [21].

3.2.2. Risk Analysis and Review (RAR)

The next phase of the business continuity management system is the risk analysis and review. This phase involves assessing risk, determining risk treatments, and formulating risk treatment strategies. Moreover, it details the analysis of risks and vulnerabilities to the organisation. This allows the organisation to determine incidental events while addressing the vulnerabilities to minimize risk and threats during the deepfake ransomware attack. The following consideration of this phase is to implement, maintain, and monitor the effectiveness of the assessed risk, control options, and cost of effectiveness, establishing key disaster scenarios [21].

3.2.3. Business Impact Analysis (BIA)

In this phase, organisations implement business impact analysis to analyse the potential impact of an incident, the effectiveness of the operational interruptions, determine the primarily functional and operational dependencies, and establish restoration priorities. This process is carried out by obtaining data on the organisation's functions, support systems, and IT applications. In this way, the obtained data is then used for validation, and to essentially determine the recovery of business operations, systems, and IT applications [6].

3.2.4. Business Continuity Strategy (BCS)

Business continuity strategy is used by an organisation to determine operational and recovery strategies to maintain and continue business operations and functions during the deepfake ransomware incidents. This is to enhance the survivability of the organisation [6].

To further elaborate, a business continuity plan needs to be established. Said plan is there to ensure the continuity of an organisation during any incident through its framework of Prevention, Preparedness, Response, and Recovery (PPRR), illustrated in Fig. (**2**) below [19].

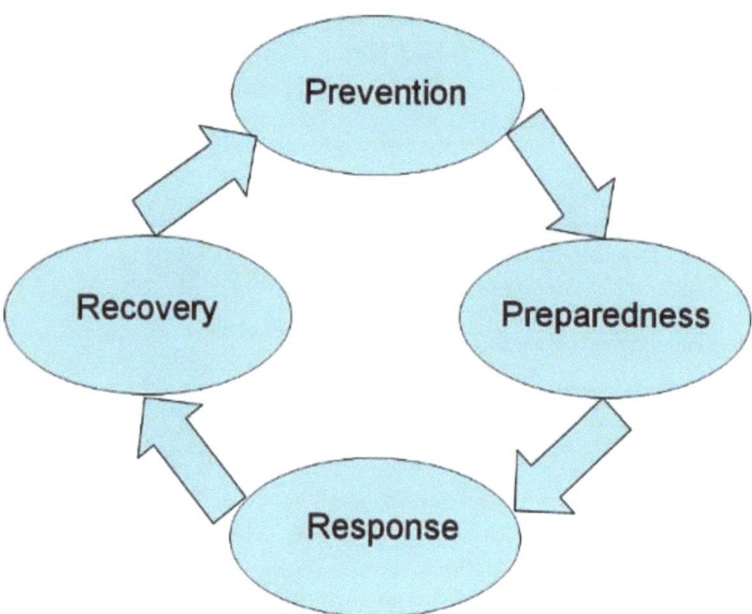

Fig. (2). Business continuity planning process [19].

3.2.5. Business Continuity Planning Process

Prevention refers to the methods and strategies adopted by the organisation to prevent the deepfake ransomware incident. This helps mitigate risk and works hand in hand with the risk management plan. This involves the organisation developing teams and departments to provide solutions to incoming attacks. Thus, reducing the impact and risk it may have on an organisation. Preparedness is the readiness of an organisation when the deepfake ransomware incident has occurred. Through the development of action and incident response plans, it is possible to determine the likely risk and attack scenarios that may occur, making the organisation prepared for an attack. Therefore, when an incident or attack has taken place, the organisation is able to respond to it immediately. Due to the organisation's preparedness, they can implement incident response plans to contain, control, and minimise the impact of an incident. Recovery is referred to the amount of lost, stolen, or destroyed data during the incident that needs to be recovered to resume business operations as usual.

3.2.6. Testing, Exercising, and Improving

For the organisation to carry out its business continuity plan effectively, the organisation must review its plans by testing, exercising, and improving its plan. This is the next phase of the business continuity management system. By testing the validity of the plan, it finds errors in the plan and improves them to be more efficient and effective. Therefore, this phase involves 3 key steps: testing, exercising, and improving [21]. Testing is referred to designing a test program to be implemented by the management and staff of the organisation. The test program details clear guidelines of tasks that need to be performed when an incident occurs. The next step is to exercise the test program. This includes the relevant teams required for exercising said test program. Thus, the result of the test will indicate faults and errors that occurred during the execution of the test program. This allows the organisation to improve its business continuity plan using findings from the test program. Hence, making the organisations business continuity plan more effective.

3.2.7. Program Management

With the emphasis on business continuity for an organisation, the project management phase ensures the survivability and recoverability of the organisation during the incident. The objective of this phase is to ensure the validity of business continuity strategy and plan development. Therefore, project management ensures that the business continuity plan is consistent with current business operations, available, accessible, and distributed to the recovery team, while also maintaining the standard, efficiency, and effectiveness. Thus, enabling a quick and effective response to an attack. Furthermore, developing advanced level testing, exercising, and improving, together with incorporating training & awareness programs, and creating a business continuity management culture for an organisation enhances the effectiveness of an organisation during an attack [29 - 32].

3.3. Disaster Recovery

Disaster recovery is the process of the organisation preparing for recovery and continuity of operations despite an attack. Disaster recovery focuses on the restoration of data and information systems that were affected during the attack. For the organisation to have successful disaster recovery, it requires a disaster recovery plan. Although business continuity plans address the facets of the organisation, the disaster recovery plan focuses on the information technology that has been affected. The plan incorporates the protection measures, analysis of critical business functions, and prevention methods. Furthermore, the plan assists the organisation in restoring serves, backups, and re-creating private branch exchanges to meet the organisation's requirements. Thus, this permits the organisation to recover the affected areas, while preventing loss of data that would result in a financial impact, loss of confidence and reputation of an organisation. Therefore, fast recovery is essential to an organisation status. Moreover, the disaster recovery plan minimises the recovery time, improves security, enhances the decision making process time, and prevents potential legal liabilities. Benefits of the disaster recovery plan: secures software and hardware data records, recovers lost data, and provides guidelines in response to attacks that ensure the organisation's continuity [9]. The disaster recovery plan consists of the following:

3.3.1. Disaster Recovery Team

The organisation employs a dedicated recovery team, who is assigned to retrieve data and ensure that the team is aware of their tasks and objectives during the incident.

3.3.2. Review Emergency Kit

Developing an emergency kit that consists of sensitive data and information, would be key for recovery. The emergency kit should be kept off-site in case of physical damage, or in an isolated offline network in case of a software or network breach.

3.3.3. Review Contact List

Having an updated contact list of shareholders, consumers, suppliers and employees during the attack, allows the organisation to use alternative methods of contacting them. This ensures that the continuity of the business is not badly affected, while the incident response from the organisation is underway [29].

3.3.4. Identifying Alternative Suppliers and Facilities

In some deepfake ransomware attacks, the business operation may come to a halt. This could be because the attack creates backlogs of orders or disruption in the production process, which in turn, leads to cancelling or pausing in operation with the parent company. Thus, by having alternative suppliers and facilities to fulfil the organisation's needs, it is able to maintain business continuity [7].

3.3.5. Includes Business Impact Analysis

As discussed earlier with the business continuity management system, the business impact analysis determines the data storage, location, and criticalness of its operations. Furthermore, with metric sets, the organisation is acknowledged by the impact of the incident and the survival of the organisation.

3.3.6. Inventory Check List of Physical Assets

With an inventory checklist of the organisation's physical assets, such as computers, servers, network hardware, and others, the recovery of the infected physical asset is made easier. Furthermore, updating all equipment to its latest versions, ensure safety and protection against future attacks [26].

3.3.7. Inventory Check List of Logical Assets

This includes a checklist of the organisation's tools, technology, software, operating systems, application programs, and others. Specification of such critical logical assets must be updated with the current versions to avoid future attacks and ensure recovery [26].

3.3.8. Communication Plan

In cases of an attack occurring after operational hours, a communication plan is needed for the incident response and disaster recovery team to act immediately during the attack. This ensures that despite the after operational hours, the organisation does not risk wasting time to defend against the attack and starts its recovery process immediately [26].

3.3.9. Data Backup Plans

During an attack, data can be stolen, lost, corrupted, or compromised. Data backup plans allow organizations to retrieve and recover damaged or compromised data. This is done by identifying the data that needs to be backed up, implementing backup procedures for hardware and software, scheduling periodic backups, and validating backed-up data. Depending on the organization's structure, data backup plans may consist of onsite and offsite data centers, cloud-based data centers, or hybrid data centers. Onsite and offsite data centers refer to the organization's infrastructure that houses its data facilities, storage, and equipment. With a cloud-based data center, the organization can virtually store its data on the cloud without the need for physical infrastructure. This allows the organization to cut costs while enabling access to data anytime and anywhere. On the other hand, some organizations use a hybrid approach, which consists of both onsite and offsite data centers, including cloud-based data centers [22].

3.3.10. Testing the Disaster Recovery Plan

With the disaster recovery plan in place, continuous testing of the plan is required. This is to ensure that any faults or errors found in the plan are mitigated and secured. Thus, constant improvement to the plan permits an effective disaster recovery plan [22].

3.3.11. AI in Disaster Recovery

With the integration of machine learning and artificial intelligence technology, it is recommended to implement such technology with the disaster recovery plan. AI technology offers the organisation self-learning and developing skills to better itself against future attacks. This is because artificial intelligence examines data sets with higher accuracy than people. Tools such as deep neural networks allow the organisation to predict potential risks and threats. With the use of business impact analysis and risk assessment systems, the implemented AI offers an insight into the weak points of the organisation and allows for further investigation. As AI is self-automated, during the disaster recovery period, the AI can automate the disaster recovery plan which allows for business continuity. Moreover, as the AI learns from past and current incidents, it improves the incident response actions and disaster recovery plans [32].

4. DEFENCE TECHNIQUES

Once the organization's business continuity strategies and disaster recovery plan have been reviewed, further improvements to security measures are needed. To improve the organization's security with defense techniques to prevent deepfake ransomware, there are a few key points that need to be taken into consideration. These include strengthening the organization's security practices in addition to relying on deepfake detection [14]. The importance of strict verification procedures must be enforced by the organization. There are various prevention countermeasures that can be implemented by the organization to further prevent attacks. Such as:

4.1. Comprehensive Data Backup and Recovery Plan

The implication of the data backup and recovery plan described earlier provides a stronger detection countermeasure. The use of whitelist applications that restrict access to authorized personnel only, can allow detection of unauthorized access, thus, making it easier for the organisation to detect malicious ware [14].

4.2. Inconsistencies

Inconsistencies that appear in data and information sharing is to be taken into consideration, because, if captured early, defence protocols are commenced as soon as possible. This helps mitigate possible deepfake ransomware attacks.

4.3. Limitation of Voice and Images

Employing strict regulations for sharing voice and image throughout the organisation's network limits the amount of data needed to create a deepfake. Hence, deepfakes require data sums of voice recordings and images to create a more believable deepfake [14].

4.4. Multi-factor Authentication

It is a tool used to provide multiple authentication factors to verify the validity of the user. Such as Google Authenticator, which implements a two-step verification process. The first is a Time-based One-time Password Algorithm and the second is HMAC-based One-time Password algorithm [10]. This reduces the likeliness of an attack to be successful, as phishing attempts to create a deepfake ransomware are foiled.

4.5. Restriction of Deepfake Tools

A restriction of deepfake tools must be in place by the organisation. This would further discourage employees to make deepfake for malicious use. Apps and tools such as ReFace and FaceSwap must be prohibited by the organisation. Furthermore, a lack of reviewing the terms and conditions of the app used could lead to the leaking of information, as some apps may sell such data to third-party sources.

4.6. Isolate Infected Devices

As soon as an attack has taken place, the infected devices must be isolated immediately. This is to prevent further damage to the organisation's network. This allows the incident response and data recovery teams to focus all their efforts on the isolated area for faster recovery and business continuity [10].

4.7. Intrusion Prevention Software

With the use of intrusion prevention software, organisations create rules that disallow any executable folders to run from Local AppData folders. Moreover, filtering .exe files sent throughout the organisation's network can prevent such files from being downloaded [14].

4.8. AI and Blockchain Detection Technology

Through automated technology, the organisation's implementation of AI as a detection software against deepfake attacks enhances the organisation's detections protocol. Moreover, cryptographic tools that generate hashes set for the organisation's media, empowers the AI software to identify the originality and altered media. Thus, mitigating against such risks is cost-efficient and effective. Furthermore, incorporating the use of blockchain enhances the detection process [9]. Blockchain is a distributed ledger, that empowers the organisation to store data online without the requirement for centralized servers. The data stored with blockchain is tamper-proof which restricts changes [5].

4.9. Content Authenticity Initiative (CAI)

As an intuitive countermeasure, Content Authenticity Initiative (CAI) defends against deepfakes. It is a system that attaches encrypted content attribution metadata tags to digital media to verify the origin of data. This proves the validity of the content, by proving it was created by a reliable source. Thus, the CAI detects the issue with the approach of content protection/copyright point of view. Furthermore, it notifies the organisation if the content has been altered [11].

4.10. Systems and Software Updates

Keeping all systems and software of the organisation allows for updates that reduce the risk of an attack. More often than none, cybercriminals take advantage of the lack of system updates, to perform attacks. This is because newer versions of updates have mitigated, overcome, and improved its systems from previous attacks [25].

4.11. Enable Anti-Virus

To further prevent malware and attacks, a reliable anti-virus is needed by the organisation. Anti-viruses monitor, detect, and prevent malware attacks. Anti-viruses provide keylogging systems that can be monitored and analysed for further prevention and detection purposes. With constant updates and monitoring by the organisation, future attacks would be reduced [25].

4.12. Server Message Block (SMB)

Such protection against ransomware is needed because network protocols and systems may be vulnerable to similar attacks. This is because the vulnerability caused by the SMB server is a buffer overflow. This gives the attackers content control through the exploits of its buffer overflow [3]. Moreover, the file-sharing firewall does not verify the code being entered, thus creating an opportunity for attackers to place malware codes *via* remote code. Most importantly, as SMB handles transactions for an organisation, it has become a vulnerability exploit. Therefore, malicious ransomware codes, inserted during transaction orders could exploit the whole system, allowing attackers to breach the organisation's systems [3]. Moreover, as this type of attack is a remote code execution attack for Windows systems, attackers can carry it out from any location. All they need is a successful penetration into the organisation's SMB servers.

There are a few SBM vulnerability bugs that need to be mitigated and addressed to reduce the risk of future ransomware to the organisation. Educating the employees of the organisation on the different types of exploits helps the organisation in preventing future ransomware attacks. Such as:

- EternalBlue: It is a bug process of converting File Extended Attributes (FEA) from OS2 structure to NT structure by the Windows SMB implementation, leading to a buffer overflow in the non-paged kernel pool. The buffer overflow is a programming flaw that allows the data to be written to a reserved memory area (the buffer) go outside of bounds (overflow), allowing it to write data to adjacent memory locations [2]. Therefore, attackers can control the content of certain memory locations that are not permitted.
- EternalRomance: This is an RCE attack that exploits CVE-2017-0145 against the legacy SMBv1 file-sharing protocol. File sharing over SMB is normally used for local networks, and the SMB ports are blocked from the Internet *via* a firewall. These exploits are a type of confusion vulnerability where verification of codes and objects is not performed through its programming flaws [2]. This allows attackers to feed function pointers or data into the wrong piece of code, which may lead to code execution.
- EternalChampion: This is a rare condition exploit in SMBv1 transactions. It is the behaviour of a system where the output depends on the sequence or timing of other uncontrollable events. This happens when the systems orders are not intended and are out of place [2].

To protect an organization's system from an SMB attack, the system must be patched. A patched system will prevent attackers from gaining access. Current updates help patch the Server Message Block vulnerabilities. Therefore, constant updates and testing of the system are required to prevent future attacks [3].

5. AWARENESS OF THE DEEPFAKES RANSOMWARE

Furthermore, providing training and education to employees in information sharing and awareness towards the deepfakes ransomware enhances the organisation's security in preventing future attacks. Educating employees about security risks and methods of prevention creates skilful employees, who are able to detect attacks [5]. The organisation is responsible for establishing security awareness and information-sharing programs. These programs bring awareness to the employees through training and educating them with awareness topics such as:

5.1. Email Scams

Email scams such as phishing emails are a form of attack that allows the attacker to gain access and vital data to carry out further attacks. With the data collected from phishing attacks, deepfake ransomware is easily created. Therefore, training employees to differentiate between legit and scam emails helps reduce the risk of an attack.

5.2. Malware

Malicious malware, which can be delivered in the form of a file and may appear to be from a trusted source, is used to steal, destroy, or compromise an organization's data and sensitive information. Precautionary methods should be followed to mitigate the potential risk. Malware that is installed may transmit data and information collected to the host attacker, providing them with ample data to create a deepfake ransomware.

5.3. Password Security

Educating employees on the importance of password security is of utmost importance. Despite the strength of the password, there is always a chance of being breached. Therefore, applying unique passwords for different accounts limits the severity of the breach. Moreover, frequent changes of passwords reduce the risk of an attack.

5.4. Removable Media

Untrusted removable media such as USBs or CDs may contain malware or viruses that execute an autorun protocol once connected to a device. Thus, awareness of the capability of untrusted removable media is important.

5.5. Safe Internet Habits

Creating safe internet habits within an organization prevents penetration attacks. Training employees to recognize suspicious and spoofed domains, the differences between HTTP and HTTPS, and not providing essential credentials to untrusted websites lessens the possibility of such attacks.

5.6. Data Management and Privacy

With the high collection of data through daily operations of the organisation, proper management of data and its privacy needs to be protected. Thus, having business data classification strategies for employees to identify, protects data at each level.

5.7. Inconsistencies

Deepfakes are not perfect, so inconsistencies make them easy to spot. With adequate training, employees of the organization can spot inconsistencies in deepfakes, such as speech rhythm, movement, blinking, lighting, skin tone, synchronization, and digital artifacts [25].

5.8. Security Protocols Act

As deepfakes created by hackers are used to make voice or video calls, establishing security protocols with specified check-up sums procedures for employees to follow when receiving such calls allows prevention of an attack [5].

5.9. Considering the Source

Employees of the organisation should fact check the source of information that is received [11]. Once employees have been educated and trained, the organisation needs to ensure that verification procedures are being followed, by having the employees receive live calls from trained professionals who emulate the tactics of real attackers [31].

CONCLUSION

In conclusion, the methods and strategies proposed to mitigate the impact and potential risks to the organisation, the implementation of risk management, business continuity and disaster recovery, improvement to the organisation security and awareness towards the attack must be carried out to limit the future risk of such an attack. Furthermore, continuous improvements to the proposed methods should be made. Therefore, to further prove the proposed implemented strategies, testing and exercising them continuously bring readiness and awareness to the organisation and its employees. Moreover, the strategies proposed, benefit the organisation by developing well-educated staff, quick.

REFERENCES

[1] "Deepfakes: How to prepare your organization for a new type of threat," Oct. 6, 2020 [Online]. Available https: //www.accenture.com/nl-en/blogs/insights/deepfakes-how-prepare-your-organization [Accessed: 15th March 2021].

[2] Arntz, P., "How threat actors are using SMB vulnerabilities," Malwarebytes Lab, Dec. 14, 2018 [Online]. Available: https://blog.malwarebytes. com/101/2018/12/how-threat-actors-are-using-smb-vulnerabilities/ [Accessed: 15th March 2021].

[3] W. Asher, "Is the deepfake phenomenon your number one cyber risk?," Feb 19, 2020 [Online]. Available: https://www.barnowl. co.za/insights/is-the-deepfake-phenomenon-your-number-one-cyber-risk/ [Accessed: 15th March 2021].

[4] Balji., "Protection Against the Server Message Block (SMB) Vulnerability Exploit | Paladion," Paladion, Aug. 22, 2019 [Online] Available: https: //www.paladion.net/blogs/protection-againsttheserver-message-block-smb-vulnerability-exploit- paladion [Accessed: 15th March 2021].

[5] Beyersdorf, M., "Deepfakes A New Threat to Organizations," Hornetsecurity, July 15, 2020 [Online]. Available: https://www.hornetsecurity.com/en/ security-information/deepfakes-threat-to-organizations/ [Accessed: 15th March 2021].

[6] P. Bryant, "Business Continuity Management and Resilience Framework." Griffith University, Dec. 3, 2018 [Online]. Available: https: //sharepointpubstor.blob.core.windows.net/policylibrary-prod/Business%20Continuity%20Management%20and%20Resilience%20Framework.pdf [Accessed: 15th March 2021].

[7] "Develop recovery strategies," July 9, 2018 [Online]. Available: https: //www.business.qld.gov.au/running-business/protecting-business/ri-k-management/recovery-plan/strategies [Accessed: 15th March 2021].

[8] "Risk management, business continuity & disaster recovery," March 18, 2019 [Online]. Available: https: //continuity2.com/business-continuity-blog/ what-are-the-relationships- between- risk-management- business- continuity -and-disaster-recovery [Accessed: 15th March 2021].

[9] "Cybersecurity Spotlight – Disaster Recovery Plan (DRP)," 2021 [Online]. Available: https: //www.cisecurity.org/spotlight/cybersecurity-spotlight-disaster-recovery-plan-drp/ [Accessed: 15th March 2021].

[10] N. Cric, "How to Protect Your Business From Deepfakes," Clutch, Sept. 25, 2019 [Online]. Available: https: //clutch.co/it-services/resources/how-to-protect-business-deepfakes [Accessed: 15th March 2021].

[11] "What is SMB vulnerability and how it was exploited to launch the WannaCry ransomware attack? Everyone," June 16, 2019 [Online]. Available: https: //cyware.com/news/what-is-smb-vulnerability-and- how-it- was- exploited -to- launch- the- wannacry -ransomware -attack-c5a97c48 [Accessed: 15th March 2021].

[12] J. Davis, "Deepfakes Cost Companies Millions, and That's Just the Beginning," HR Daily Advisor, Aug 22, 2019 [Online]. Available: https: //hrdailyadvisor.blr.com/2019/08/22/deepfakes-cos--companies-millions-and-thats-just-the-beginning/ [Accessed: 15th March 2021].

[13] C. Daly, "Why Deepfakes Pose An Unprecedented Threat To Businesses", AI Business, para. 2, Jan. 5, 2019. [Online] Available: https: //aibusiness.com/document.asp?doc_id=760904 [Accessed: 15th March 2021].

[14] P. Dialani, "Best Ways to Prevent Deepfakes," Analytics Insight, Oct. 5, 2020 [Online]. Available: https: //www.analyticsinsight.net/best-ways-prevent-deepfakes/ [Accessed: 15th March 2021].

[15] U. Aslam, M. Jayabalan, H. Ilyas, and A. Suhail, "A survey on opinion spam detection methods", *Int. J. Scient. Technol. Res.,* vol. 8, no. 9, 2019.

[16] A. Drozhzhin, "How to mitigate the impact of deepfakes," Kaspersky Daily, March 12, 2020 [Online]. Available: https: //www.kaspersky.com/blog/rsa2020-deepfakes-mitigation/34006/ [Accessed: 15th March 2021].

[17] B. Edwards, "Fake video threatens to rewrite history. Here's how to protect it," Fastcompany, Oct. 3, 2020 [Online]. Available: https: //www.fastcompany.com/90549441/how-to-prevent-deepfakes [Accessed: 15th March 2021].

[18] J. Efron, "How Deepfakes Deceptions are Affecting Businesses," ShuftiPro, Dec 19, 2019 [Online] Available: https: //shuftipro.com/blog/how-deepfakes-deceptions-are-affecting-businesses [Accessed: 15th March 2021].

[19] M. Foerster, and C. Arnold, "Firm Business Continuity Planning and Risk Mitigation Strategies," IFAC, Sept. 24, 2019 [Online]. Available: https: //www.ifac.org/knowledge-gateway/preparing-futu-e-ready-professionals/discussion/firm-business-continuity-planning-and-risk-mitigation-strategies [Accessed: 15th March 2021].

[20] O. Giudice, L. Guarnera, and S. Battiato, "Fighting deepfakes by detecting GAN DCT anomalies," arXiv, Jan. 24, 2021 [Online]. Available: https: //arxiv.org/abs/2101.09781 [Accessed: 15th March 2021].

[21] M. Goh, "Business Continuity Management Planning Methodology," BCM Institute, March 1, 2019 [Online]. Available: https: //blog.bcm-institute.org/blog/bcm-planning-methodology [Accessed: 15th March 2021].

[22] T. Hanna, "Top 4 Types of Disaster Recovery Plans," Solutions Review, Oct 29, 2018 [Online]. Available: https: //solutionsreview.com/backup-disaster-recovery/top-three-types-of-disaster-r-covery-plans/ [Accessed: 15th March 2021].

[23] R. Howard, "How to protect yourself from deepfake scams," Ting Blog, Aug. 17, 2020 [Online] Available: https: //ting.com/blog/deepfake-scams/ [Accessed: 15th March 2021].

[24] A. Johansen, "Deepfakes: What they are and why they're threatening," US.Norton.com, July 24, 2020 [Online]. Available: https: //us.norton.com/internetsecurity-emerging-threats-what-are-deepfakes.html [Accessed: 15th March 2021].

[25] J. Kietzmann, L.W. Lee, I.P. McCarthy, and T.C. Kietzmann, "Deepfakes: Trick or treat?", *Bus. Horiz.,* vol. 63, no. 2, pp. 135-146, 2020. [http://dx.doi.org/10.1016/j.bushor.2019.11.006]

[26] E. MacDonald, "Cyber Attacks on Small Businesses on the Rise," Foxbusiness.com, April 27, 2016 [Online]. Available: https: //www.foxbusiness.com/features/cyber-attacks-on-small-businesses--n-the-rise [Accessed: 15th March 2021].

[27] G. Murphy, and E. Flynn, "Deepfake false memories", *Memory,* vol. 30, no. 4, pp. 1-13, 2021. [PMID: 33910482]

[28] K. Puzon, "Fight Cyber Crime with Business Continuity," Expedient, July 29, 2015 [Online] Available: https: //expedient.com/knowledgebase/blog/2015-07-29-fight-cyber-crime-with-b-siness-continuity/ [Accessed: 15th March 2021].

[29] E. Rexhepi, "How Can an Effective Disaster Recovery Plan Help Your Business?," PECB Insights, Dec. 1, 2016 [Online]. Available: https: //insights.pecb.com/can-effective-disaster-recovery-plan-

help-business/ [Accessed: 15th March 2021].

[30] "Disaster Resilience Business Continuity Management Framework," Oct. 2019 [Online]. Available: https: //www.sahealth.sa.gov.au/wps/wcm/connect/3c1dd486- a699- 45ea- 9718-850062743ced/SAHealth_ Disaster_ Resilience_ Business_ Continuity_ Mgt_ Framework_ v3.2_FINA....pdf?MOD=AJPERES&CACHEID=ROOTWORKSPACE-3c1dd48--a699-45ea-9718-850062743ced-nwMEBT2 [Accessed: 15th March 2021].

[31] "Deepfakes: How to Defend Yourself from Attack," Security Boulevard, May 20, 2020 [Online]. Available: https: //securityboulevard.com/2020/05/deepfakes-how-to-defend-yourself-from-attack/ [Accessed: 15th March 2021].

[32] A. Wilson, "5 ways AI can help in disaster protection and recovery," Tech Talks, Oct. 4,2019 [Online]. Available: https: //bdtechtalks.com/2019/10/04/artificial-intelligence-disaster-recovery/ [Accessed: 15th March 2021].

CHAPTER 7

Use of Machine Learning in Credit Card Fraud Detection

Manoj Jayabalan[1*] and **Shiksha**[1]

[1] *School of Computer Science and Mathematics, Liverpool John Moores University, Liverpool, UK*

Abstract: Credit card fraud is a growing concern, and it poses a significant threat as individual information is being misused and causing a substantial monetary loss. Hence, the prevention of credit card fraud is crucial. Credit card fraud detection is used to differentiate the transactions, either as legitimate or fraudulent. Recently, different machine learning techniques have been implemented to detect credit card fraud. However, the main challenge with fraud detection is that the credit card data is highly skewed, with the fraudulent transactions as less as 1% of the total data. This study investigates the performance of the four supervised machine learning algorithms: logistic regression, support vector machine, decision tree, and random forest, along with different sampling techniques to better understand the fraud detection attributes and performance measures associated with it. This review is also concentrated on exploring different works where the model has a better value for all of the performance evaluation metrics: Recall, precision, F1-score, accuracy, MCC, AUC, and area under the precision-recall curve. This will detect credit card fraudulent transactions better and control credit card fraud.

Keywords: Decision tree, Logistic regression, Random undersampling technique, Random forest, Random oversampling technique, Supervised machine learning algorithms, SVM, SMOTE.

1. INTRODUCTION

Organisations dealing with money are the soft targets for fraudulent activities. Fraud is an illegitimate effort to get information from anyone (internal and external threat) who is acquainted with the system and the security measures through various means [1 - 3]. According to Shift Processing, more than 24 billion dollars were lost in 2018 due to credit card fraud [4]. A credit card is a payment card issued by a financial institution to the cardholder to make purchases with

* **Corresponding author Manoj Jayabalan:** School of Computer Science and Mathematics, Liverpool John Moores University, Liverpool, UK; E-mail: m.jayabalan@ljmu.ac.uk

Muhammad Ehsan Rana & Manoj Jayabalan (Eds.)

ease [5]. The rapid growth of e-commerce has led to a large increase in the use of credit cards, which has become a necessity of financial services [6].

Online usage of credit cards is an easy target for fraudsters, as it does not require the physical presence of the card [7]. As the operation of credit cards is increasing, there is a higher chance of people (other than the cardholder) misusing it for their own interest. This intentional and illegal misuse of someone's card or its information without their knowledge for attaining financial help to cause loss is termed as credit card fraud [6]. The technology that credit card companies utilises to detect fraud cases is known as a fraud detection system (FDS). The main goal of an FDS is to reduce the false alarm rate and maximise accuracy [8]. The FDS should be quick in action, and the credit card should be immediately revoked once the fraud is detected [9].

Numerous studies have shown machine learning algorithms for credit card fraud detection [9 - 14]. The selection of a suitable algorithm is a complex step towards building the model, and it should always be selected according to the required condition. Hence, the purpose is to review the existing studies using different supervised machine learning techniques on the highly skewed dataset. This will help in better detecting the fraudulent transaction as well as controlling the credit card fraud. The rationale to explore the four techniques selected in this paper: logistic regression, support vector machine, decision tree, and random forest is because of their performance values and advantages reported in the different literatures. Moreover, not many papers have compared the result of all four techniques in a single work, so this work focuses mainly on said algorithms, comparing the performance of the classifiers based on accuracy, sensitivity, specificity, precision and AUC.

2. CONTROL LAYERS IN CREDIT CARD FRAUD DETECTION SYSTEM

In the real world, credit card transactions are inspected rapidly using machine learning algorithms to investigate the transactions and to generate the alert for the sceptical records. These alerts are inspected to know whether it is a genuine or a fraud case, after which feedback is provided as a label for that transaction. It is a significant challenge to investigate every instance of sceptical records due to the time and cost factor. Additionally, these transactions will be unlabelled if customers are not reporting for these transactions. It is stated that this problem, coined as verification latency, has been ignored by several researchers, and it has also been assumed that the labelling of each transaction is done continuously for the fraud detection system [12, 13]. Fig. (**1**) represents a formal design of the real-world fraud detection system with its main features [13]. It is observed that layers

1-4 have been implemented automatically, whereas the last layer requires human interference.

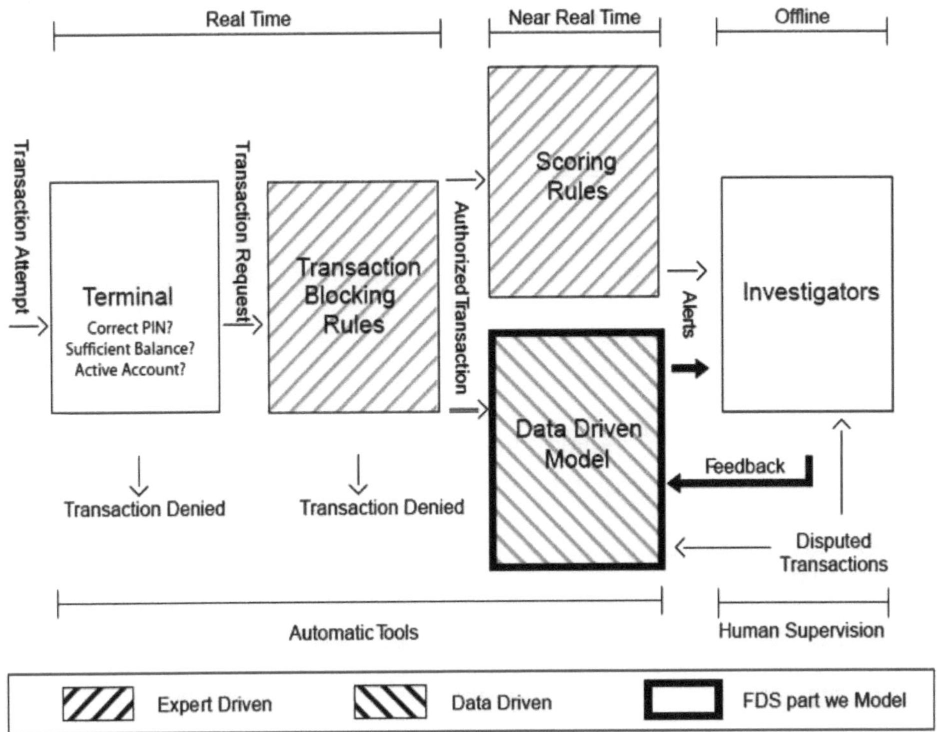

Fig. (1). Control layers used in the fraud detection system [13].

Control layers used in the fraud detection system:

- Terminal: It is the first layer of control for fraud detection and carries out all the required safety measures for all the transaction instances. Such instances include: pin code, card status, number of attempts for accessing credit card, and balance. The response for the online transaction should be in real-time, in milliseconds of time, while the terminal gets details for that particular card from its issuing organisation. If the instances lack any of these details, the transaction is declined. In the case of a successful event, it is passed on to the second layer of control.
- Transaction blocking rules: It is the second layer of control that comes in action after the request is passed from the terminal. These rules are like if-(then)-else conditions, which are used to revoke the fraud transactions. These rules work on

a small number of the available information in the event of a transaction event and do not analyse user behaviour or profile. Many transaction blocking rules are implemented at the same time, and those transactions which launch any of them are revoked. The important point here is that the transaction is revoked. However, the card is not blocked after the execution of this step. These rules are modelled manually and are known as expert-driven components of the fraud detection system. These rules should be rapid in action, accurate, and error-free so that not all legitimate transactions are blocked. The transaction requests after passing this step are approved to further proceed to the third layer of control.

- Scoring rules: It is the third layer of control for FDS and expert-driven components, which are like if-(then)-else conditions, similar to the transaction blocking rules. The only difference of scoring rules compared to the transaction blocking rules is that it works on the aggregated features (derived from the original features), and a score is given to all the approved transactions. A higher score represents a higher probability of fraud transactions.
- Data-driven model: This is the data-driven component, and a machine learning algorithm or classifier can be implemented to detect the fraud. This is done by estimating the probability of the aggregated features. The data-driven model layer is analysed using the labelled transactions. Different classifiers and sampling techniques can be implemented to get an efficient data-driven model. The main aim of the data-driven model is to generate highly accurate alerts.
- Investigators: They are the experts in investigating the transactions for the credit card and manage the expert-driven components of the fraud detection system. Investigators are responsible for developing transaction blocking rules as well as scoring rules.

The investigators generate alerts for the sceptical records using the scoring rules and the data-driven model. The existing studies focus mainly on the data-driven component of the fraud detection system, and a discussion regarding the same is presented in section 14.3.

3. TYPES OF CREDIT CARD FRAUD DETECTION SYSTEM

Fraud detection for the credit card is used to distinguish the successful transactions as legitimate or fraudulent ones. The fraud detection techniques for credit card transactions are mainly categorised into two groups shown in Fig. (**2**) fraud analysis. This is also known as misuse detection and user behaviour analysis, also referred to as anomaly detection.

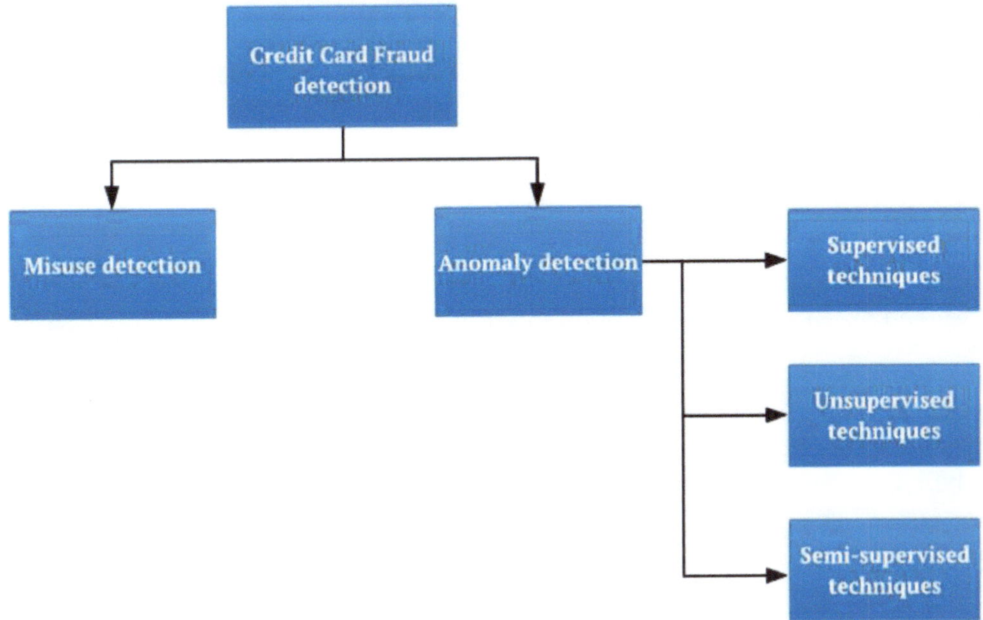

Fig. (2). Types of credit card fraud detection.

In the misuse detection approach, the fraud detection system trains on both legitimate and fraudulent transactions. This makes it a simple and quick fraud detection method as it searches for the familiar fraud pattern on which the model is trained. Hence, it can identify the known frauds [3]. However, since it only searches for the known patterns of misuse, it lacks the potential to identify the novel frauds [3].

Anomaly detection or outlier detection method is utilised by the fraud detection system, and it depends on the user behavioural profile. It is the process of distinguishing the suspicious observations from the rest of the given information [15]. This technique models the user behavioural profile and analyses it for any changes from the historical pattern [10, 11, 16-19]. It is further categorised into three groups: supervised, unsupervised, and semi-supervised techniques [3]. This study only focuses on anomaly detection.

3.1. Machine Learning Techniques

As it can be seen in Fig. (**2**), anomaly detection is further classified into supervised, unsupervised, and semi-supervised techniques. Supervised fraud detection works on estimating the models based on the legitimate and fraudulent transactions in the given data, classifying the new transactions as one of them and predicting the probability of fraudulent transactions for the given data [10]. In the supervised learning techniques, the credit card dataset is used to generate the classification models based on the transaction output label. The models are then used to predict the label for the new transaction as a fraud or a genuine. The main advantage of supervised methods is that all the result outputs provided by the supervised machine learning algorithms are relevant to the human being which can be utilised for data classification and regression [3]. The supervised methods suffer from higher costs for labelling all the datasets. The important supervised techniques are logistic regression, support vector machine, decision tree, random forest, and neural networks [6].

Unsupervised fraud detection works on identifying the unusual transaction, also known as outliers, and predicting the probability of fraud cases for the given transaction data [20]. In unsupervised machine learning algorithms, a transaction is labelled as fraud if it is different from the customer's normal account behaviour, otherwise, it is a genuine transaction. Since no previous labelled output data is used, it is known as unsupervised techniques. The main advantage of using the unsupervised method is that there is no cost for labelling as no output label is used. The different types of unsupervised machine learning techniques used for credit card fraud detection are detailed in this paper [21].

These methods are between supervised and unsupervised ones, with a few labelled data, as well as a high number of unlabelled data [3]. The semi-supervised technique models use both labelled and unlabelled samples. Labelling the data for supervised techniques needs a high cost for the skilled human intervention or the required experiment, whereas unlabelled data is rather inexpensive. For such scenarios where cost matters, semi-supervised learning techniques can be useful and practical. The unlabelled data, in combination with the labelled ones can result in improved performance for the model. Since the work presented in this study is for supervised methods, the study of unsupervised and semi-supervised techniques is kept out of scope and not discussed in this paper.

3.2. Selection of Suitable Techniques for Credit Card Fraud Detection

As the financial industry deals with a large number of fraud-labelled transactions, supervised fraud detection performs better than unsupervised ones [14, 22]. To differentiate between said techniques, the supervised methods detect fraud cases with low false-positive rates. No alarm is fired for no-fraud cases in the test dataset; hence false positive (FP) rate is lowered significantly. Nevertheless, these models learn from previously labelled datasets. If this dataset is limited or has specific fraud data, it is difficult to detect the new type of fraud, which means that the false negative (FN) rate can be high. On the other hand, the unsupervised methods perform better for detecting the new types of frauds as it does not look for any fraud pattern and is not being trained with previously labelled datasets. Even though unsupervised techniques perform better for detecting novel frauds, these methods experience a high number of false alarms [6]. Hence, a selection of suitable techniques are subjected to the given condition. The goal of all methods is to reduce FP and FN rates whilst, at the same time, increasing the true positive and true negative rates with good overall accuracy [6].

Several machine learning algorithms have been experimented on the ULB machine learning credit card dataset to get the best performance which will be investigated here. Since the dataset is highly biased, some works have utilised the sampling method to balance the data, while many of them have not used any balancing techniques. Moreover, for such a highly skewed dataset, the accuracy is not the right performance metric to get the best result. Hence, other performance metrics are being evaluated by the different experiments [10]. The balancing techniques and the machine learning algorithms with different performance metrics used in each work have been collated in the Discussion section for better understanding.

Several papers have compared the supervised and unsupervised machine learning techniques for ULB dataset. The experiment result showed that the supervised algorithms performed slightly better than the unsupervised methods giving the better prediction result, whereas [8] stated that no models are less than the other models in performance. This paper concludes that if the data is very small, then it is better to go with unsupervised algorithms, as it will save time and labour. Labelling the data in supervised methods consumes more time and labour costs. Many studies have focused on the supervised algorithms for ULB datasets [11, 16, 18, 19, 23 - 30]. Among those works, many have concluded that Random forest outperforms other supervised techniques [11, 19, 26, 28, 29]. Few works also demonstrated logistic regression, achieving the best performance [18, 30]. This paper demonstrated SVM providing the best results followed by logistic regression [24]. It has identified the important features of the ULB dataset, which shows better accuracy for credit card fraud detection [24]. It has utilised featuring engineering on the original dataset to study the feature ranking. The paper concluded that ULB dataset has no difference in performance than the raw and feature selected datasets as the given dataset is already transformed using PCA [28].

The random forest performs most accurately for detecting the normal transactions but misclassifies the fraud cases, whereas the neural networks detect the fraud cases well but misclassify the normal ones [27]. An ensemble method combining the random forest and neural networks is proposed to provide the best result for the ULB dataset. Without using a sampling technique, the accuracy is very high for this heavily skewed dataset. However, there is a high chance of mistaking many fraudulent transactions as genuine ones. For the fraud detection of credit cards, the main goal is to reduce the misclassification of the fraudulent cases, and secondly, aim to reduce the misclassification of the genuine cases [27]. High accuracy with high precision and Recall is achieved using this ensemble, which demonstrates a high value for the ensemble method classifiers [27].

4. CREDIT CARD FRAUD DETECTION CHALLENGES

The design of effective fraud detection techniques can minimise the financial loss to the organisation. However, it suffers from three primary hurdles: non-stationarity, skewness, and assessment. Often times, fraudsters mimic the cardholders spending behaviour, which makes the profiles of the fraudster and cardholder alike (non-stationarity data distributions). These changing dynamics between genuine and fraudster profiles is known as the concept of drift, making it particularly challenging for machine learning algorithms to accurately predict fraudulent transactions [9, 31 - 34]. One study has shown the static and online learning approach to handle the non-stationarity issues. A static learning approach is a method where the detection is developed from scratch in a period of time (for example: once in a month or year). In comparison, the online learning method is improved continuously on the arrival of new data [9].

The second challenge faced in designing a fraud detection system is dealing with the class imbalance issue in the data since genuine transactions outnumber fraudulent ones. Credit card fraud datasets, therefore, have extreme class imbalance issues, as fraudulent transactions typically account for less than 1% of the total transactions [9, 10]. This is an important area of study as the positive case (fraudulent case) is hard to distinguish and becomes even harder with the inflow of data, where the representation of such cases decrease even further. Traditional machine learning algorithms work on the assumption of equal class distribution and equal cost of misclassification, so it is up to the researchers to devise a workaround for a balanced learning approach [11, 17].

Numerous studies have shown various sampling techniques to tackle the imbalance problem and implement accurate prediction models aimed at improving the detection rate of fraudulent transactions [9, 10, 12, 14, 35]. Synthetic Minority Oversampling Technique (SMOTE) creates new synthetic instances of the minority class using KNN. Synthetic instances that are created using this technique have been shown to perform better in several studies [7, 9, 35]. Some studies have shown the drawbacks of oversampling and under-sampling by implementing various machine learning algorithms and evaluating the performance using precision and Recall. It was found that oversampling suffers from overfitting, and under-sampling ignores some of the useful data [36]. In [17], the implementation of complex sampling methods showed the best performance for random forest with an AUC of 91.48% and the worst for SVM with an AUC of 88.77% [17].

The detection of credit card fraud is classified as a cost-sensitive problem where there is an associated cost incurred for incorrectly classifying a genuine transaction as fraudulent and incorrectly classifying a fraudulent transaction as genuine [10]. Therefore, assessment (evaluation metrics) is an important aspect of the fraud detection system in order to understand the performance of the model. The accuracy metric for evaluating a model is not suitable for datasets with class imbalance, as it would bias the model towards the majority class since the accuracy metric calculates the total of correct predictions. The Area under the Curve (AUC), Sensitivity (also referred to as Recall), Precision, and F1 score are the most commonly used evaluation metrics in the existing studies [37].

5. DISCUSSION

The fraud detection system can be made effective by overcoming the issues associated with it. The main problem with the credit card fraud detection reported in all the literatures is the high skewness of the dataset with fraud transactions as low as 1% of the total data. Hence, the distribution of data is always biased towards the no-fraud cases. This biased dataset leads to an uncertain fraud detection process where even if the classifier is not good enough, it will give a high accuracy of 99%, which is unacceptable [10, 11, 16 - 19]. And when the machine learning techniques are unable to work perfectly on the unbalanced dataset, problems arise in terms of credit loss and poor customer service [24]. Whenever a fraud transaction is wrongly detected as a genuine one, the loss is to be borne by the credit card companies and customers. In comparison to whenever a no-ssfraud is misclassified as a fraud one, the loss is to the customer in terms of bad service.

To overcome this, a sampling technique is utilised for both legitimate and fraudulent transactions in order to obtain a decent class distribution [10, 11, 16 - 19]. Random oversampling of minority class and random under-sampling of majority class are the most commonly used balancing techniques for credit card fraud detection, having a better performance compared to other resampling methods. It also showed that the under-sampling performance outmatched the oversampling method for the larger number of data so it is mostly preferred for huge datasets.

Whenever a credit card transaction is made, many features like transaction amount, date, summary of account, minimum payment, and transaction fees are generated. A single transaction is insufficient to explore the credit card pattern, so a larger number of transactions are needed to analyse the credit card behaviour [9]. But due to sensitivity and confidentiality issues, it is very difficult to have the real-world dataset to work on [10, 11, 16 - 19].

Numerous research has compared the supervised techniques with unsupervised ones [10, 16, 19, 26, 28, 38]. Few kinds of research have been done for reducing the false alarms for credit card fraud detection using support vector machines [39, 40]. The good performance of the fraud detection system comes with the disadvantage of having a higher number of false alarms. This means the credit card company does not want to restrict its customers frequently, even though it wants to minimise the losses due to fraud. Numerous research has compared the supervised techniques with unsupervised ones [10, 16, 19, 26, 28, 38].

As the bank industry deals with a large number of fraud-labelled transactions, supervised fraud detection performs better than unsupervised ones [14, 23]. The supervised methods detect fraud cases with low false-positive rates. No alarm is fired for no-fraud cases in the test dataset hence false positive (FP) rates are lowered significantly. However, since these models learn from the previously labelled dataset, and if this dataset is limited or has specific fraud data, it is difficult to detect the new type of fraud, which means that the false negative (FN) rate can be high. In contrast, the unsupervised methods perform better for detecting the new types of frauds as it does not look for any fraud pattern and is not trained with the previously labelled dataset. Even though unsupervised techniques perform better for detecting novel frauds, these methods experience a high number of false alarms [6]. Thereby, the selection of suitable techniques is subjected to the given condition. The goal of all methods is to reduce FP and FN rates, and at the same time, increase true positive and true negative rates with good overall accuracy.

The suitable technique being supervised and unsupervised for any problem is always selected as per the conditions required. As no output labels are used for unsupervised methods, the machine detects the hidden characteristic of the dataset itself, making the unsupervised method inferior to the supervised one [41]. Generally, all financial organisations trade in high numbers of fraud-labelled transactions, resulting in the supervised methods being preferred for the fraud detection of credit cards [14, 22].

The purpose of the fraud detection system is to boost the correct predictions and lower the wrong ones that are maximising the accuracy while minimising the false alarm rate [1]. There is always a chance that the identified fraud transaction is, in fact, a genuine one or vice versa. Although the detection of no-fraud transactions as fraud ones may work, since fraud cases are further investigated, misclassifying a fraud transaction as no-fraud will have a severe effect on the fraud detection system. Hence, a good performance of FDS should have a low number of false positives and negative rates [10, 26].

Comparing various machine learning algorithms, it is asserted that the logistic regression and random forests perform better with high values of accuracy, sensitivity, and specificity [10, 26]. The random forest is found to have the best performance values in comparison to other methods in many papers [9, 13, 42].

Table **1** summarises the literatures about the sampling methods, evaluation metrics, and the results obtained for the reported studies. All these works have been implemented on the credit card dataset of ULB machine learning using different supervised machine learning techniques. The under-sampling is denoted as US and over-sampling as OS in Table (**1**). The several works demonstrate random forest and logistic regression achieving the best performance followed by the decision trees and support vector machine. The evaluation metrics column shows various performance measures utilised for the different works other than accuracy.

Table 1. Comparison of different reviewed literature works.

Papers	Sampling Method	Evaluation Metrics	Results
[22]	US	AUROC	Random forest, AUROC 98.8%
[8]	Not used	Specificity, sensitivity, precision and balanced accuracy	Logistic regression
[9]	SMOTE	AUC, Precision	Random forest
[13, 14, 35]	SMOTE, US	ROC curve, sensitivity, specificity and G-mean	Decision tree
[10]	-	Accuracy, sensitivity, specificity, precision	Random forest, accuracy 96.2%, sensitivity 72.7%, specificity 98.7% precision 86%
[25]	Hybrid	Sensitivity, specificity, accuracy	KNN, decision tree, Logistic regression same performance
[26]	Not used	Accuracy, sensitivity, specificity, precision	Random forest, accuracy of 98.6%

(Table 1) cont.....

Papers	Sampling Method	Evaluation Metrics	Results
[43, 44]	US	Sensitivity, specificity,(FPR), (MCC) and balanced classification rate (BCR)	Decision tree
[13, 42]	US	ROC curve and average precision	Random forest
[19]	US	Accuracy, TPR, FPR, G-mean, Recall, precision, specificity and F1-score	Random forest
[28]	Not used	Pearson correlation coefficient	Decision tree
[45]	Not used	Accuracy, precision, Recall, F-measure	Logistic regression
[27]	Not used	Accuracy and precision and Recall	Ensemble, accuracy of 99.95% with precision of 85.85% and Recall of 86.73%
[37]	Not used	ROC, Savings	Decision tree
[7, 46]	SMOTE	Accuracy	All gave same accuracy
[39, 40]	Not used	Accuracy	Accuracy 94.3% customers accurately with 13.3% good customers as bad and 6.7% bad customers as good ones
[47]	Not used	Accuracy	Decision tree
[16]	Hybrid	Accuracy, sensitivity, specificity, precision, Matthews's correlation coefficient and balanced classification rate	NaA_ve Bayes
[11]	US	Accuracy, Recall, precision and area under curve (AUC)	Logistic regression accuracy of 93.9% and AUC of 94%
[29]	US and OS	Accuracy, sensitivity, specificity and precision	Random forest with accuracy of 98.6%, sensitivity of 98.4%, specificity of 90.5% and precision of 99.7%
[17]	SMOTE	Precision and Recall and AUC	Random forest with AUC of 91.48%
[18]	US	Accuracy, precision, Recall, f1-score and support	Logistic regression accuracy of 93.6%
[30]	OS	Accuracy	Logistic regression
[24, 48]	Not used	Sensitivity and specificity Matthews Correlation coefficient (MCC)	Support vector machine MCC 0.813 & accuracy 99.937%

CONCLUSION

It is inferred from the above discussion that almost all the papers are either not using the sampling method or utilising only one of the sampling techniques for credit card fraud detection, which has already been fixed before implementing the model. Very few papers have compared the sampling techniques for better performance; hence this has motivated me to go ahead in this work to compare different sampling techniques with different machine learning algorithms.

From the above discussion, it is found that the highest accuracy of 99.95% is achieved for credit card fraud detection. But as discussed, only the accuracy is not a sufficient measure for such a highly biased dataset; other parameters should also have maximum value along with accuracy. But, Table **1** shows that the model has a high accuracy of 99.95% with lower precision and Recall. Additionally, from the above discussion, it is concluded that if sensitivity or specificity is increased, accuracy decreases. As seen, for a high value of accuracy of 98.6%, a specificity of only 90.5% is achieved. Moreover, there are no models which have high values for accuracy, sensitivity, specificity, and AUC. The literature review presented above showed that the high-performance metrics are mostly given by models: random forest and logistic regression. Hence, the purpose of this study is to develop a model that achieves better values compared to the results obtained in the literature review for all the mentioned evaluation metrics. Furthermore, a comparative analysis of four supervised machine learning techniques: logistic regression, SVM, decision tree, and random forest, on the highly skewed real-time dataset will be done for better detecting the credit card fraudulent transaction as well as controlling the credit card fraud. The performance of the classifiers will be compared based on accuracy, sensitivity, specificity, precision, AUC, and area under precision and recall curve. As the credit card fraud data is highly biased, this work enhances the handling of the highly biased credit card fraud dataset as presented in related papers by using different methods of sampling.

The significant challenge for implementing and deploying in the hypermarket will cost heavily on the hardware component and system development. This is because the gateway used in the system is relatively expensive, and a microcontroller is needed for every product shelf in the hypermarket to make the system fully functional. Scheduled maintenance on the IoT devices also needs to be done by hypermarket staff to allow the system to perform its best at all times.

Moreover, the system's graphic user interface (GUI) must be made viewable on different devices, which means it has to be dynamically changing the location of the GUI element according to the device's viewport and screen resolution. Besides that, the connectivity such as Wi-Fi and Bluetooth inside the hypermarket must remain to stay online during opening hours to prevent a sensor from being left out; that may result in reducing the accuracy of the stock management. Some other signal interferences, such as customers' mobile phones or any other electronic device which will continuously be pulsing electromagnetic waves, may also affect and deteriorate the connectivity in the hypermarket's sales floor.

REFERENCES

[1] Yufeng Kou, Chang-Tien Lu, S. Sirwongwattana, and Yo-Ping Huang, "Survey of fraud detection techniques", *Conf. Proceeding - IEEE .Int .Conf ,Networking Sens*", *Control,* vol. 2, no. February, pp. 749-754, 2004.
[http://dx.doi.org/10.1109/ICNSC.2004.1297040]

[2] P.R. Shimpi, and M.A. Pavaskar, "Survey on Credit Card Fraud Detection Techniques", *Int. J. Eng. Comput. Sci.,* vol. 2, no. 11, 2016.
[http://dx.doi.org/10.18535/Ijecs/v4i11.25]

[3] A. Abdallah, M.A. Maarof, and A. Zainal, "Fraud detection system: A survey", *J. Netw. Comput. Appl.,* vol. 68, pp. 90-113, 2016.
[http://dx.doi.org/10.1016/j.jnca.2016.04.007]

[4] S. Processing, "Credit Card Fraud Statistics," Shift Processing, 2020. [Online]. Available: https://shiftprocessing.com/credit-card-fraud-statistics/

[5] B. Finserv, "What is Credit Card?," Bajaj Finserv, 2018. [Online]. Available: https://www.bajajfinserv.in/what-is-credit-card

[6] Z. SamanehSorournejad, and R. Zojaji, "A survey of credit card fraud detection techniques", *Data and Technique Oriented Perspective,* pp. 1-26, 2016.

[7] D. Varmedja, M. Karanovic, S. Sladojevic, M. Arsenovic, and A. Anderla, "Credit Card Fraud Detection - Machine Learning methods," 2019 18th Int. Symp. INFOTEH-JAHORINA, INFOTEH 2019 - Proc., no. October, pp. 1–5, 2019, doi: 10.1109/INFOTEH.2019.8717766.
[http://dx.doi.org/10.1109/INFOTEH.2019.8717766]

[8] S. Mittal, and S. Tyagi, "Performance evaluation of machine learning algorithms for credit card fraud detection", *Proc. 9th Int. Conf. Cloud Comput. Data Sci. Eng. Conflu.,* pp. 320-324, 2019.
[http://dx.doi.org/10.1109/CONFLUENCE.2019.8776925]

[9] A. Dal Pozzolo, O. Caelen, Y.A. Le Borgne, S. Waterschoot, and G. Bontempi, "Learned lessons in credit card fraud detection from a practitioner perspective", *Expert Syst. Appl.,* vol. 41, no. 10, pp. 4915-4928, 2014.
[http://dx.doi.org/10.1016/j.eswa.2014.02.026]

[10] S. Bhattacharyya, S. Jha, K. Tharakunnel, and J.C. Westland, "Data mining for credit card fraud: A comparative study", *Decis. Support Syst.,* vol. 50, no. 3, pp. 602-613, 2011.
[http://dx.doi.org/10.1016/j.dss.2010.08.008]

[11] S. Rajora, "A Comparative Study of Machine Learning Techniques for Credit Card Fraud Detection Based on Time Variance", *Proc. 2018 IEEE Symp. Ser. Comput. Intell. SSCI 2018,* pp. 1958-1963, 2019.
[http://dx.doi.org/10.1109/SSCI.2018.8628930]

[12] F. Carcillo, A. Dal Pozzolo, Y.A. Le Borgne, O. Caelen, Y. Mazzer, and G. Bontempi, "SCARFF : A scalable framework for streaming credit card fraud detection with spark", *Inf. Fusion,* vol. 41, pp. 182-194, 2018.
[http://dx.doi.org/10.1016/j.inffus.2017.09.005]

[13] A. Dal Pozzolo, G. Boracchi, O. Caelen, C. Alippi, and G. Bontempi, "Credit card fraud detection: A realistic modeling and a novel learning strategy", *IEEE Trans. Neural Netw. Learn. Syst.,* vol. 29, no.

8, pp. 3784-3797, 2018.
[http://dx.doi.org/10.1109/TNNLS.2017.2736643] [PMID: 28920909]

[14] I. Mekterovi, L. Brki, and M. Baranovi, "A systematic review of data mining approaches to credit card fraud detection", *WSEAS Trans. Bus. Econ.,* vol. 15, pp. 437-444, 2018. Corpus ID: 55202073

[15] A. Gupta, "Machine Learning for Anomaly Detection," GeeksforGeeks, 2018. [Online]. Available: https://www.geeksforgeeks.org/machine-learning-for-anomaly-detection/

[16] J.O. Awoyemi, A.O. Adetunmbi, and S.A. Oluwadare, "Credit card fraud detection using machine learning techniques: A comparative analysis", *Proc. IEEE Int. Conf. Comput. Netw. Informatics, ICCNI* pp.1-9, 2017.
[http://dx.doi.org/10.1109/ICCNI.2017.8123782]

[17] M. Puh, and L. Brki, "Detecting credit card fraud using selected machine learning algorithms", In: *42nd International Convention on Information and Communication Technology, Electronics and Microelectronics (MIPRO),* Opatija, Croatia. pp.1250-1255, 2019.
[http://dx.doi.org/10.23919/MIPRO.2019.8757212]

[18] A. Kumar, "Fraud Detection in Online Transactions Using Supervised Learning Techniques". In: Towards Extensible and Adaptable Methods in Computing, Springer Singapore, 2018.

[19] S. Dhankhad, E.A. Mohammed, and B. Far, "Supervised machine learning algorithms for credit card fraudulent transaction detection: A comparative study", *Proc. 2018 IEEE 19th Int. Conf. Inf. Reuse Integr. Data Sci. IRI 2018.*
[http://dx.doi.org/10.1109/IRI.2018.00025]

[20] R. J. Bolton, and D. J. Hand, "Unsupervised profiling methods for fraud detection", *Proc. Credit Scoring Credit Control VII,* vol. Sep 5, pp. 235-55, 2001.
[http://dx.doi.org/10.1.1.24.5743]

[21] R.J. Bolton, and D.J. Hand, "Unsupervised Profiling Methods for Fraud Detection", *J. Chem. Inf. Model.,* vol. 53, no. 9, p. 287, 2008.
[http://dx.doi.org/10.1017/CBO9781107415324.004]

[22] X. Niu, L. Wang, and X. Yang, *A Comparison Study of Credit Card Fraud Detection: Supervised versus. Unsupervised*, 2019.

[23] X. Niu, L. Wang, and X. Yang, *Adv. Artif. Intell.,* 2019. "A Comparison Study of Credit Card Fraud Detection: Supervised *versus* Unsupervised."

[24] K. Randhawa, C.K. Loo, M. Seera, C.P. Lim, and A.K. Nandi, "Credit Card Fraud Detection Using AdaBoost and Majority Voting", *IEEE Access,* vol. 6, pp. 14277-14284, 2018.
[http://dx.doi.org/10.1109/ACCESS.2018.2806420]

[25] D. Dighe, S. Patil, and S. Kokate, "Detection of Credit Card Fraud Transactions Using Machine Learning Algorithms and Neural Networks: A Comparative Study", *Proc. 2018 4th Int. Conf. Comput. Commun. Control Autom. ICCUBEA* 2018, pp. 1–6, 2018.
[http://dx.doi.org/10.1109/ICCUBEA.2018.8697799]

[26] K. Navanshu, and Y.S. Saad, "Credit Card Fraud Detection Using Machine Learning Models and Collating Machine Learning Models", *J. Telecommun. Electron. Comput. Eng.,* vol. 118, no. 20, pp. 825-838, 2018.

[27] I. Sohony, R. Pratap, and U. Nambiar, "Ensemble learning for credit card fraud detection", *ACM Int. Conf. Proceeding Ser.* pp.289-294, 2018.
[http://dx.doi.org/10.1145/3152494.3156815]

[28] O.A. John, A. Adebayo, and O. Samuel, "Effect of Feature Ranking on the Detection of Credit Card Fraud: Comparative Evaluation of Four Techniques,",*i-manager(tm)s J. Patt. Recog., vol. 5, no. 3* p. 10, 2018.
[http://dx.doi.org/10.26634/jpr.5.3.15676]

[29] A.H. Nadim, I.M. Sayem, A. Mutsuddy, and M.S. Chowdhury, *Analysis of Machine Learning Techniques for Credit Card Fraud Detection.*, 2020, pp. 42-47. [http://dx.doi.org/10.1109/iCMLDE49015.2019.00019]

[30] S.W. Wen, and R.M. Yusuf, "Predicting Credit Card Fraud on a Imbalanced Data", *Int. J. Data Sci. Adv. Anal. Predict.,* vol. 1, no. 1, pp. 12-17, 2019.

[31] J.O. Awoyemi, A.O. Adetunmbi, and S.A. Oluwadare, "Credit card fraud detection using machine learning techniques: A comparative analysis", *Proc. IEEE Int. Conf. Comput. Netw. Informatics, ICCNI 2017* pp.1-9, 2017. [http://dx.doi.org/10.1109/ICCNI.2017.8123782]

[32] A. Dal Pozzolo, G. Boracchi, O. Caelen, C. Alippi, and G. Bontempi, "Credit card fraud detection and concept-drift adaptation with delayed supervised information", *Proc. Int. Jt. Conf. Neural Networks,* vol. 2015-Septe, 2015. [http://dx.doi.org/10.1109/IJCNN.2015.7280527]

[33] C. Jiang, J. Song, G. Liu, L. Zheng, and W. Luan, "Credit Card Fraud Detection: A Novel Approach Using Aggregation Strategy and Feedback Mechanism", *IEEE Internet Things J.,* vol. 5, no. 5, pp. 3637-3647, 2018. [http://dx.doi.org/10.1109/JIOT.2018.2816007]

[34] A. Correa Bahnsen, D. Aouada, A. Stojanovic, and B. Ottersten, "Feature engineering strategies for credit card fraud detection", *Expert Syst. Appl.,* vol. 51, no. January, pp. 134-142, 2016. [http://dx.doi.org/10.1016/j.eswa.2015.12.030]

[35] Di. S. Sisodia, N. K Reddy, and S. Bhandari, "Performance evaluation of class balancing techniques for credit card fraud detection", *IEEE Int. Conf. Power, Control. Signals Instrum.,* pp. 2747-2752, 2018. [http://dx.doi.org/10.1109/ICPCSI.2017.8392219]

[36] Z. Z.-H, Liu Xu-Ying, and Wu. Jianxin, "Exploratory undersampling for class-imbalance learning", *Lect. Notes Comput. Sci,* vol. 39, no. 2, pp. 539-550, 2009. [http://dx.doi.org/10.1007/978-3-642-34478-7_71]

[37] A.C. Bahnsen, D. Aouada, A. Stojanovic, and B. Ottersten, "Detecting credit card fraud using periodic features", *2015 IEEE 14th International Conference on Machine Learning and Applications (ICMLA),* Miami, FL, USA, pp. 208-213, 2015. [http://dx.doi.org/10.1109/ICMLA.2015.28]

[38] A. Dal Pozzolo, "Adaptive Machine Learning for Credit Card Fraud Detection Declaration of Authorship", PhD Thesis, no. December, p. 199, 2015. [http://dx.doi.org/10.14419/ijet.v7i2.9356]

[39] N. Demla, and A. Aggarwal, "Credit card fraud detection using svm and reduction of false alarms", *Int. J. Innovation. Eng. Technol (IJIET),* vol. 7, no. 2, pp. 176-182, 2016.

[40] M. Kamboj, and S. Gupta, "Credit Card Fraud Detection and False Alarms Reduction using Support Vector Machines", *Int. J. Adv. Res.,* vol. 2, pp. 1-10, 2016.

[41] S. Mehndiratta, and K. Gupta, "Credit Card Fraud Detection Techniques: A Review", *Int. J. Comput. Sci. Mob. Comput.,* vol. 8, no. 8, pp. 43-49, 2019.

[42] V. Van Vlasselaer, C. Bravo, O. Caelen, T. Eliassi-Rad, L. Akoglu, M. Snoeck, and B. Baesens, "APATE: A novel approach for automated credit card transaction fraud detection using network-based extensions", *Decis. Support Syst.,* vol. 75, pp. 38-48, 2015. [http://dx.doi.org/10.1016/j.dss.2015.04.013]

[43] M. Fahmi, A. Hamdy, and K. Nagati, "Data mining techniques for credit card fraud detection: Empirical study", *Sustain. Vital Technol. Eng. Informatics,* vol. 2015, pp. 1-9, 2016.

[44] Y. Sahin, and E. Duman, *Detecting Credit Card Fraud by Decision Trees and Support Vector*

Machines. vol. I. IMECS, 2011.

[45] O.S. Yee, S. Sagadevan, and N.H.A.H. Malim, "Credit card fraud detection using machine learning as data mining technique", *J. Telecommun. Electron. Comput. Eng.,* vol. 10, no. 1-4, pp. 23-27, 2018.

[46] Z. Kazemi, and H. Zarrabi, "Using deep networks for fraud detection in the credit card transaction", pp. 630–633, 2017. [http://dx.doi.org/10.1109/KBEI.2017.8324876]

[47] P. Save, P. Tiwarekar, K. N, and N. Mahyavanshi, "A Novel Idea for Credit Card Fraud Detection using Decision Tree", *Int. J. Comput. Appl.,* vol. 161, no. 13, pp. 6-9, 2017. [http://dx.doi.org/10.5120/ijca2017913413]

[48] V.B. Nipane, P.S. Kalinge, D. Vidhate, K. War, and B.P. Deshpande, "Fraudulent Detection in Credit Card System Using SVM & Decision Tree", *IJSDR,* vol. 1, no. 5, p. 590, 2016.

SUBJECT INDEX

A

B

Muhammad Ehsan Rana & Manoj Jayabalan (Eds.)

C

D

E

F

G

H

I

T

U

V

W